"I encourage broad use of *The New Anabaptists*. It builds on the foundations of the early Anabaptist movement by reporting how current believers in new places and in new ways are sharing their faith and practices. We may see many churches declining, but Stuart Murray's book helps us see it emerging in new, creative ways. This book gives me hope for the future of the Anabaptist church in post-Christendom."

PALMER BECKER, speaker, pastor, church planter, missionary, educator, and author of *Anabaptist Essentials*

"Offering an excellent companion volume to his earlier book *The Naked Anabaptist*, Stuart Murray's *The New Anabaptists* fleshes out the faith practices that characterize emerging Anabaptist (and Anabaptist-adjacent) communities. Murray offers a refreshing articulation of how Anabaptist theology might translate into the real-world experience of Christ followers in a variety of contemporary settings. This vision will be appealing to scholars, clergy, students, and laity alike as it inspires dreams for how an Anabaptist faith might be practiced in the twenty-first century."

MELANIE HOWARD, associate professor of biblical and theological studies and chair of the Biblical and Religious Studies division at Fresno Pacific University

"As I read *The New Anabaptists*, I kept remembering the moments when my children entered this world: it was fraught with danger, full of pain, noisy, messy, and full of apprehension—yet those were among the most beautiful and life-giving moments of my existence. Such is the nature of the core practices that Stuart Murray describes when lived out: they can be difficult, there are dangers to watch out for, and we may experience apprehension—yet when we put them into practice, we also experience the life-giving Spirit of God. This book will likely challenge something about the way that you live, but any challenge rooted in leading us closer to Jesus is worth the discomfort it may cause."

KEVIN WIEBE, senior pastor of New Life Christian Fellowship in Stevenson, Ontario, and author of *Faithful in Small Things*

"What a thoughtful, honest, and practical resource for those yearning for authentic neo-Anabaptist expressions of Christian life! Here is a vision of what such a life might look like, grounded in actual communities and their accounts of struggle as well as joy of being part of something life-giving and life-transforming. While particular in its focus and context, this book will be an inspiration to many, not only in Britain and Ireland but also far beyond."

REV. DR. LINA TOTH, theologian, educator, and author of *Singleness and Marriage After Christendom*

"The church in the West faces an identity crisis that has us reaching for a way of being church that matters more in our lives and to the world. Here is a timely call to take stock in this liminal space, seeking an ancient way that can point us to a more Jesus-centered, collaborative, generous, honest, peace-filled, and just expression of the faith. Stuart Murray and his colleagues humbly offer a winsome description of shared practices for Anabaptist Christians that can form emerging and existing Christian communities toward a renewed identity and witness for our time."

DAVID BOSHART, president of Anabaptist Mennonite Biblical Seminary

"In this thought-provoking book, Stuart Murray Williams explores the outworking of Anabaptist convictions and values through specific practices, and three further chapters written by practitioners demonstrate how both values and practices are being expressed in specific situations. Inspiring and practical, *The New Anabaptists* will be invaluable for individuals and communities seeking to be faithful followers of Jesus today."

LINDA WILSON, chair of Anabaptist Mennonite Network

"A number of Jesus followers in Britain and Ireland have been courting Anabaptism for several decades. More recently they have strengthened that relationship by 'announcing their engagement' through a set of Anabaptist-inspired common practices and by undertaking new peacemaking and church planting initiatives. This is their story. If you are wondering what vibrant, authentic, and local Anabaptist life and witness might look like in their post-Christendom context and other settings like it, this book should rise to the top of your reading list."

JAMES R. KRABILL, visiting professor at Anabaptist Mennonite Biblical Seminary and Dallas International University

THE
NEW
ANABAPTISTS

THE
NEW
ANABAPTISTS

PRACTICES FOR EMERGING COMMUNITIES

Stuart Murray

Author of *The Naked Anabaptist*

WITH CONTRIBUTIONS BY

Alexandra Ellish | Karen Sethuraman | Juliet Kilpin

HERALD
P R E S S

Harrisonburg, Virginia

Herald Press
PO Box 866, Harrisonburg, Virginia 22803
www.HeraldPress.com

Library of Congress Cataloging-in-Publication Data
Names: Murray, Stuart, 1956- author. | Ellish, Alexandra, contributor. |
  Kilpin, Juliet, contributor. | Sethuraman, Karen, contributor.
Title: The new Anabaptists : practices for emerging communities / Stuart
  Murray ; with Alexandra Ellish, Karen Sethuraman, and Juliet Kilpin.
Description: Harrisonburg, Virginia : Herald Press, [2024] | Includes
  bibliographical references.
Identifiers: LCCN 2023040498 (print) | LCCN 2023040499 (ebook) | ISBN
  9781513812984 (paperback) | ISBN 9781513812991 (hardcover) | ISBN
  9781513813004 (ebook)
Subjects: LCSH: Anabaptists. | Communities--Religious aspects--Anabaptists.
  | BISAC: RELIGION / Christian Church / Growth | RELIGION / Christian
  Ministry / Pastoral Resources
Classification: LCC BX4931.3 .M874 2024 (print) | LCC BX4931.3 (ebook) |
  DDC 284/.3--dc23/eng/20231023
LC record available at https://lccn.loc.gov/2023040498
LC ebook record available at https://lccn.loc.gov/2023040499

Study guides are available for many Herald Press titles at www.HeraldPress.com.

THE NEW ANABAPTISTS
© 2024 by Herald Press, Harrisonburg, Virginia 22803. 800-245-7894. All rights reserved.
Library of Congress Control Number: 2023040498
International Standard Book Number: 978-1-5138-1298-4 (paperback);
    978-1-5138-1299-1 (hardcover); 978-1-5138-1300-4 (ebook)
Printed in United States of America

28 27 26 25 24   10 9 8 7 6 5 4 3 2 1

CONTENTS

FOREWORD

While living in London, England, in the 1990s, I had the privilege of coediting a small, photocopied magazine called *Anabaptism Today* with Stuart Murray. I was a Mennonite with Swiss ancestry extending back to the early Anabaptists. Stuart, new to Anabaptism, was a visionary who saw better than anyone how the Anabaptist impulse could inspire church renewal in a post-Christian society. I constantly learned from Stuart—not just facts, but a way of adapting Radical Reformation insights for relevant contemporary mission.

It is easy for persons attracted to the Anabaptist tradition to romanticize its early expressions or to describe the movement in idealistic terms. Academic study of church history is essential, and Stuart has ably done his share. But the power of the presentation in *The New Anabaptists* is the author's lifelong passion to put ideas from this Reformation legacy into practice at street level. If other portrayals of Anabaptism are lofty or abstract, this book has all the dust, bustle, and struggle of real faith communities.

The New Anabaptists, companion to Stuart's earlier book *The Naked Anabaptist*, is a resource for all God's people, including Mennonites, Brethren, Baptists, and others seeking

useful models for contemporary Christian witness. The "treasure in a field" that Stuart and other new Anabaptists have uncovered is not an ethnic subculture but a Jesus-centered counterculture. Anabaptism at its best points us to the life, death, and resurrection of the Lamb of God. Though thoroughly trinitarian, new Anabaptists put emphasis on the *life and teaching* of Jesus. They sometimes draw applications that challenge or unsettle long-established institutional church patterns. Faithful praxis for them is just as important as faithful belief.

I was among twentieth-century North American Mennonite missioners to the United Kingdom who believed that we should not launch a new denomination there. Rather, we wanted to encourage Jesus-centered discipleship and peacemaking in already established church traditions. But now I am persuaded by the assessment of Stuart and colleagues that Britain has become so overwhelmingly secular and multireligious that the time is right for church planting.

This book is a report from the church-planting test plots that emerged from that decision. These missional seed beds are not imports to the United Kingdom, but local expressions of the Holy Spirit. The embryonic faith communities featured here are experimental and small, but their vision is expansive. Descriptive rather than prescriptive, this book is candid about struggles of church planting and evangelism at the margins of society. It also captures the energy and joy of vision for the reign of God taking root and bearing fruit.

The cultural specificity of this book, which puts British "clothing" on our shivering naked Anabaptist, adds to its strength. With loneliness and social fragmentation increasing in the Western world, new Anabaptists embody a church that features hospitality, belonging, and engagement. North

Americans, being perhaps a generation behind the United Kingdom in becoming post-Christian, have much to learn from this story. Pioneers of neo-Anabaptist mission in the United Kingdom can inspire and inform similar experimentation elsewhere in the world.

The wisdom in this book is nuanced with Stuart's characteristic humility and understatement. Instead of featuring case studies of his own leadership at the culmination of the book, he has invited three other new Anabaptists to tell their stories. A mentor to many around the world, Stuart speaks with gentle authority, drawing from decades of missional leadership. Together, these pioneers of neo-Anabaptist mission in the United Kingdom can inspire and inform similar experimentation in other cultures. What gets served up in this volume is a welcome harvest for all who want to draw from new Anabaptist test plots for a vision of how God may be shaping our churches in the future.

—J. Nelson Kraybill
President, Mennonite World
Conference (2015–2022)
President, Anabaptist Mennonite
Biblical Seminary (1996–2009)
Author of *Stuck Together: The Hope
of Christian Witness in a Polarized
World*

ACKNOWLEDGMENTS

One of the challenges facing anyone writing a book is to identify the sources of ideas that have found their way into it. Direct quotations can be cited and significant conversations, seminars, lectures, or books can be gratefully acknowledged, but it is not possible to remember every source of inspiration. Ideas that seemed the author's own in the process of writing might have their origins in a long-forgotten conversation or a book that does not feature in the notes. So, while I gladly acknowledge here some of those who I know contributed to this book, I am sure there are others who unwittingly did so, to whom I am also grateful.

The steering group of what was then the Anabaptist Network first suggested that we needed to identify practices alongside our core convictions. Simon Woodman, one of the members of this group, wisely advised us to designate them as "common" rather than "core" practices, so that they would not be offered as prescriptive but would encourage contextual creativity. Martin Parkes, Peter Atkins, and Alexandra Ellish formed a working group that talked together over several months and presented an initial list of practices for consideration. About thirty members of the network spent a weekend

in March 2020 reflecting on this list and refining it. I am grateful to all of these people for their contributions. I hope what I have written here builds faithfully and creatively on the foundations they laid.

I am grateful to staff at Herald Press for their positive response to my initial proposal and their assistance throughout the publishing process. I valued the comments and encouragements of others who also read the manuscript: Lloyd Pietersen, Linda Wilson, Barney Barron, Lynsey Heslegrave, and Sian Murray Williams. Helpful also were suggestions from Mennonite Mission Network mission workers to whom I presented material from the book at their retreat in France in April 2023. And I am especially grateful to my three colleagues Juliet Kilpin, Karen Sethuraman, and Alexandra Ellish—not only for their contributions to this book, but for their friendship over many years, the creative and courageous initiatives they have taken, and their thoughtful reflections on the embodiment of the practices discussed in this book.

INTRODUCTION

Clothing the Naked Anabaptist

Since the publication of *The Naked Anabaptist* in 2010, I have often been asked if I planned to write a sequel. Several possible titles have been suggested, seriously or in jest, including "Clothing the Naked Anabaptist." Until quite recently, I had been unconvinced. But developments among British and Irish Anabaptists in the past few years have changed my mind.

The Naked Anabaptist was unexpectedly popular in North American Mennonite and Church of the Brethren circles.[1] But not all reviewers were as enthusiastic as many of those who contacted me directly to express their appreciation. A few reviewers seemed a little put out that a British non-Mennonite should presume to offer such a summary of Anabaptist convictions—although some of these subsequently acknowledged that they were won over by the book's contents. Others helpfully pointed out deficiencies that I tried to correct in the second edition. However, many members of Mennonite, Mennonite Brethren, and Church of the Brethren churches bought the book, read it themselves, and discussed it in study groups or in Sunday school. I was especially encouraged to hear from

quite a number of mostly young adults who had "grown up Mennonite" but had dropped out of their churches, often because of cultural rather than theological discomfort. It seems that the book resonated deeply with them, gave them a fresh perspective on the Anabaptist vision, and stimulated a renewed commitment to discipleship.

If the impact of *The Naked Anabaptist* in North America was surprising, so too were requests to translate the book into other languages. Before long it was available in French, German, Spanish, Swedish, Korean, Japanese, and Indonesian, and I was invited to explore its themes and application at conferences around the globe.

But the book was written for the British context—to introduce the Anabaptist tradition to Christians who had stumbled across it and to reflect on the "core convictions" that had emerged from conversations within the Anabaptist Network.[2] These convictions represent a contextual adoption of the Anabaptist vision in a post-Christendom Western society by neo-Anabaptists.[3] The book's title was, of course, a misnomer—there is no such thing as a "naked Anabaptist," any more than theology, missiology, or ecclesiology can ever be devoid of cultural influences. But the title indicated an attempt to strip away cultural accretions that had inevitably grown up around the Anabaptist vision in the Mennonite circles from which we had learned so much through the long-term presence in the UK of North American mission workers.[4]

One review in a British journal especially intrigued me. I knew the reviewer, who had enthusiastically endorsed an earlier book of mine, *Post-Christendom*, but we had not spoken together about Anabaptism, as far as I can recall. The gist of his review was that the convictions expounded in the book were not Anabaptist but simply Christian. I remember being

rather uncertain how to interpret this. His perspective aligned with a comment I have often made when teaching on Anabaptism and included in the final chapter of *The Naked Anabaptist*: "Our interest is not in Anabaptism for its own sake, but in a tradition that helps us become more faithful followers of Jesus."[5] In that sense, I was tempted to agree with the reviewer.

But my experience of British Christianity over the past forty years, during which time I have taught in at least thirty-five different denominations, is that the theology, values, and ethos of the Anabaptist core convictions are by no means as widely known and embraced as this reviewer suggested. Many continue to baptize infants. Very few acknowledge that "peace is at the heart of the gospel" or prioritize peacemaking within their understanding of mission. Mutual accountability is rarely discussed or taught, let alone practiced, and consensual approaches to decision-making are not common. The implications of post-Christendom are becoming more familiar, even if they are not yet resulting in the theological, institutional, ecclesial, and missional renewal that is required, but the Anabaptist tradition has explored these implications in much greater depth than most others. And most churches do not operate with a consistent Christ-centered hermeneutic that influences their approach to ecclesial and ethical issues. The core convictions, it seems, are not "simply Christian," if by this is meant they are widely understood and embraced.

Nevertheless, the Anabaptist vision has undoubtedly captured the imagination of many British and Irish Christians over the past four or five decades. Those who would identify themselves unreservedly as Anabaptists may still be a tiny minority, but many more draw gratefully on Anabaptist perspectives. Some have embraced these values and practices instinctively and only later discovered their Anabaptist

provenance. Others have encountered Anabaptism first through books, not least in the After Christendom series commissioned and promoted by the Anabaptist Mennonite Network.[6] Still others have encountered the Anabaptist vision through relationships and conversations and have been intrigued, challenged, and inspired. The network facilitates connections and provides many resources via its website and an online journal, *Anabaptism Today*. For those interested in digging deeper, there are study groups, a theology forum, and the Centre for Anabaptist Studies.[7]

Throughout this book, the term *neo-Anabaptist* will be used for followers of Jesus in contexts without a significant historical Anabaptist or Mennonite presence who have been inspired by the Anabaptist vision to shape their discipleship and communities in relation to this vision. These are the "new Anabaptists." The emergence and growth of neo-Anabaptism in the UK and elsewhere owes a great debt to North American Mennonite mission workers, and we continue to learn from Mennonite expressions of the Anabaptist tradition (as will be evident throughout this book). But there is now an autonomous Anabaptist movement in the UK, reinterpreting and reapplying the Anabaptist tradition in ways that resonate with our post-Christendom context.

The core convictions have proved their worth over the past thirty years, but recently we have recognized that we need to go further. What practices do these convictions inspire? How do they shape communities and initiatives? There are implications in the convictions themselves, and we will frequently refer back to these and to their exposition in *The Naked Anabaptist*. But several factors have provoked us to identify some "common practices" that are likely to characterize emerging Anabaptist communities or projects. The most significant

factor has been our growing unease with the disembodied nature of Anabaptism in our context. Anabaptism is an ecclesial and communal tradition. It is not well represented by a dispersed network of individuals. We have struggled to know how to answer most of those who ask us where they can find their nearest Anabaptist church.

We understand why a succession of North American mission workers chose not to plant Mennonite churches in the UK.[8] They were concerned that doing so would appear competitive and would likely hinder their ability to interact with other Christian communities and share their distinctive insights and resources. Until very recently, we endorsed this perspective and understood our role in a similar way. As a result, although the Anabaptist Mennonite Network is small compared with many other organizations, the Anabaptist tradition is now widely known and valued across a wide spectrum of British Christianity.

But we have now embarked on church planting. In a missional context of declining numbers and the closure of many congregations (exacerbated by the fallout of pandemic restrictions), opportunities abound for non-competitive church planting. If, as we suspect, Anabaptism is unusually well-suited to contribute to a post-Christendom culture, we believe we have a responsibility to participate and to explore fresh possibilities. So, in 2020, the Anabaptist Mennonite Network launched a project, Incarnate, with a mandate to encourage the planting of missional communities with Anabaptist convictions and practices.[9] This project is at a very early stage, as indicated by the term *emerging communities* in the subtitle of this book, but it represents a significant change in our understanding of what we might contribute to the discovery of creative ways of being church and engaging in mission in our

post-Christendom society. We are also journeying with and supporting some existing churches that are eager to embrace such convictions and practices.

In addition, the network is supporting other projects with Anabaptist foundations, the most significant of which at this point is Peaceful Borders, an initiative that "seeks to accompany and equip people responding to forced migration through accompanying peacemakers, building capacity, campaigning for peace, and developing people and practice."[10]

The gradual emergence of these self-consciously Anabaptist churches and initiatives requires us, we believe, to be more explicit about the practical implementation of the Anabaptist vision and the convictions that have undergirded the development of the Anabaptist Mennonite Network. We need to clothe the naked Anabaptist!

We have chosen the term *common practices* to avoid being unduly prescriptive and to encourage contextual sensitivity. The practices explored in the first section of this book are indicative, likely to characterize Anabaptist communities and projects in our context. They are also tentative, offered for experimentation and reflection. Unlike the core convictions that have stood the test of time (although we continue to talk about possible revisions), these common practices were only formulated in 2020 and have yet to be widely endorsed or thoroughly tested. Our hope is that these common practices will offer some guidance to emerging Anabaptist communities, and that in turn, these communities will help us reflect on these practices and refine them in light of experience.

The second section of the book contains three case studies, written by my colleagues who are involved in Anabaptist initiatives, explaining how the common practices are helping to shape their activities. These case studies are all set in the British and

Irish context. In addition, in the first section, there are several references to Urban Expression, an Anabaptist-oriented mission agency that deploys and supports mission partners in marginalized urban neighborhoods.[11] Urban Expression began in 1997 and is an earlier initiative inspired by the Anabaptist vision.

Unlike *The Naked Anabaptist*, which was intended for the British context but was read much more widely, this book has a broader intended readership. It will hopefully resource the development of Anabaptist communities and projects in the UK—and perhaps also in other neo-Anabaptist contexts. But I hope it might also inform and inspire North American Mennonite readers, including those who read the earlier book, encouraging them with stories of the embodiment of their own tradition in new contexts, and inviting them to discover fresh ways of embodying this tradition in their own, many of which are moving rapidly in the direction of post-Christendom.

This book, then, is an extended reflection on the common practices, an invitation to discuss their congruence with Anabaptism and how they might be embodied, and a resource for those who are pioneering Anabaptist churches in the UK and maybe elsewhere. It is no more intended to be definitive than was *The Naked Anabaptist*, and it retains the sense of vulnerability and openness to challenge and correction. My hope is that it will stimulate conversations and inspire creative and courageous action.

UNCOVERING COMMON PRACTICES

The notion of Anabaptist common practices lends itself to a *descriptive* account, but determining the boundaries of this account is not straightforward. We could attempt to catalog and reflect on the significance of practices that frequently, albeit not always, characterize communities that have been shaped and inspired by the Anabaptist vision. We could exclude those practices that are evident within most or all Christian communities, whatever traditions they draw from, and concentrate on those that are distinctive to communities with Anabaptist convictions. Or we could examine these widely shared practices—such as singing, prayer, preaching, the Lord's Supper, governance, and witness—and investigate whether there are unusual features of these practices evident in communities rooted in Anabaptist convictions.

Our account might focus on contemporary communities, although the diversity of these communities within a global movement would make this challenging as well as enlightening. It would help us, though, to appreciate the influence of cultural contexts on ecclesial and missional practices. Alternatively, we might take our lead from the practices of the earliest Anabaptists, although we have only limited access to some aspects of their communities and we will again encounter considerable diversity. Or we might delve into the five-hundred-year history of the communities that emerged from the first generation— Mennonite, Hutterite, Amish, Brethren, and others who, like the early Anabaptists and contemporary communities, were influenced by their cultural and political contexts, as well as by their theological convictions. Will we find in all of these eras and contexts practices that are ubiquitous enough to be designated as Anabaptist common practices?

Another option is to offer a *prescriptive* approach, reflecting on the Anabaptist vision and its core convictions and suggesting that certain practices are congruent with this vision, whether or not they are currently operative. If we are working with the notion of common practices, rather than "core practices," we will not advocate a fixed or comprehensive list of such practices or attempt to define too precisely what they might involve, but instead will argue that authentically Anabaptist communities should at least be characterized by several of these practices.

Whichever approach we adopt, the practices of a community are not exclusively shaped by its stated core convictions; they are also influenced by many other factors, including precious traditions, any ethnic diversity, its socioeconomic and cultural context, varying styles of leadership, personal and corporate experiences (good and bad), past conflicts, and present priorities. Just as there is no such thing as a "naked Anabaptist," there are no practices in Anabaptist-oriented communities that are unclothed by such factors.

Our focus in this book, then, is on the embodiment of the Anabaptist vision in post-Christendom societies in neo-Anabaptist communities and initiatives, especially but not exclusively in the UK, in the third decade of the twenty-first century. The following chapters do not pretend to describe practices that characterize, or should characterize, the global Anabaptist movement. They examine practices that are already apparent in Anabaptist groups in the UK or may be adopted by those who are planting or nurturing Anabaptist communities. As in *The Naked Anabaptist*, we will pay attention to what we know of the practices of the sixteenth-century Anabaptists to provide a historical foundation for contemporary practices. This is essential if we are to avoid the temptation to construe "Anabaptist" to endorse our own preferences. But our main interest is in uncovering and examining practices that might express Anabaptist core convictions authentically in our own missional and ecclesial context.

MENNONITE AND NEO-ANABAPTIST PERSPECTIVES
Others have, of course, attempted to distill the practices of Anabaptist communities with which they are familiar and

have explored their significance. Four examples from the past twenty years, which reflect the authors' North American Mennonite cultural and ecclesial context (but perhaps not the perspectives of Asian, Hispanic, or African American or other Black Mennonites in North America) are *Following in the Footsteps of Christ: The Anabaptist Tradition* (2004) by C. Arnold Snyder; *Dissident Discipleship: A Spirituality of Self-Surrender, Love of God, and Love of Neighbor* (2006) by David Augsburger; *Practices: Mennonite Worship and Witness* (2009) by John D. Roth; and *Anabaptist Essentials: Ten Signs of a Unique Christian Faith* (2017) by Palmer Becker. Not surprisingly, many of the practices they identify overlap with those we will observe or advocate in the UK context, but it will be interesting to note some differences and omissions.

Snyder's book is a contribution to the Traditions of Christian Spirituality series, presenting the Anabaptist tradition alongside many others in a wide-ranging collection. As the book's inclusion in this series indicates, the primary focus is on spirituality, but the title of the book points toward the expression and embodiment of Anabaptist spirituality in various practices rooted in the life and teaching of Jesus. These include repentance, renunciation, readiness to suffer, following Jesus, believers baptism, admonition, communion, footwashing, living the Bible, communal worship, song, economic practices, truthfulness, and nonviolence. A very significant omission is any account of Anabaptist missional practices.[12]

Augsburger's book contains eight chapters, all of which have headings that explicitly refer to practices. These practices are radical attachment, stubborn loyalty, tenacious serenity, habitual humility, resolute nonviolence, concrete service, authentic witness, and subversive spirituality. They are outworkings of a particular understanding of spirituality, which the author denotes as "tripolar" (with God, self, and others as the three poles). The connection between spirituality and discipleship evident in Snyder's book is also apparent in this one, albeit presented in a different way and illustrated by many stories and examples. There is also a more developed missional dimension.[13]

Roth's book, part of a trilogy on beliefs, stories, and practices, draws on his wide experience of American Mennonite churches and focuses on the interaction of dimensions of worship and witness. He writes: "Christian practices are attitudes and actions—consciously nurtured in the context of the church and infused by the presence of the Holy Spirit—that make Christ's presence visible in the world."[14] Roth explores the missional significance of familiar liturgical and community activities and encourages intentionality and deeper reflection on these practices.

Becker's book overlaps with *The Naked Anabaptist* as well as this book in that it introduces both convictions and practices. His three foundational convictions are that "Jesus is the center of our faith," "community is the center of our life," and "reconciliation is the center of our work." Under these headings he discusses nine convictions or practices: discipleship, a Christocentric hermeneutic, the lordship of Jesus, forgiveness, communal discernment, accountability, reconciliation to God, reconciliation to each other, and reconciliation of conflicts. A final chapter focuses on the work of the Holy Spirit as essential in discipleship and helpfully asks what North American Mennonites might learn from Christians in the Global South.[15]

Augsburger and Roth include many illustrative stories that enliven their accounts and demonstrate the importance of the practices they describe, and all the authors to varying degrees refer to the practices of previous generations, not least the sixteenth-century Anabaptists. Nor is it surprising that many of the practices these books present are familiar within most other Christian traditions. Anabaptist communities may infuse these practices with somewhat different meanings or may experience them in significantly different ways, but (despite the claim in the subtitle of Becker's book) few are peculiar to Anabaptism.

These four books have much in common, not only in their identification of specific practices, but also in their insistence that spirituality and discipleship or worship and witness are integrally connected. This integration is refreshing in light of some older Anabaptist writings that have prioritized ethics over spirituality and also the tendency in Mennonite circles to downplay or elide the charismatic dimension of their heritage. Despite a final chapter in *The Naked Anabaptist* that underscored the relationship between discipleship and spirituality, that book and the core convictions it explored attracted criticism for giving inadequate attention to the role of the Holy Spirit, which was so important to the early Anabaptists. I hope to make more explicit in this book the relationship between the practices we will explore and the work of the Spirit.

BROADENING THE CONVERSATION

While I deeply appreciate all four of these books and have learned much from them, I am left with some misgivings. This unease is related to my limited experience of Mennonite congregations in North America. As a British neo-Anabaptist who had been inspired by the Anabaptist vision over the past decade, my first experience of American Mennonites in 1994 was disappointing and disconcerting. The Mennonite congregations I visited seemed almost indistinguishable from Protestant churches (albeit they did not display American flags).

While I recognized certain echoes of what I had assumed to be Anabaptist practices, these bore little relationship to the radicality and dynamism I associated with the early Anabaptists. Furthermore, most of the Mennonites I encountered on these visits were financially comfortable if not wealthy, mainly living in middle-class neighborhoods, seemingly content with traditional expressions of church, and very wary of engaging in any form of evangelism. Subsequent visits to North America have exposed me to a much wider range of congregations and many impressive activities beyond congregational meetings. These visits have resulted in enduring friendships that I value highly, but they also confirmed some of my initial impressions.

These comments are not meant to be dismissive or unduly critical but rather are intended as an honest appraisal from a neo-Anabaptist who deeply values the Anabaptist tradition and is enormously grateful for those communities that have embodied and sustained its convictions and values over nearly five hundred years. British Anabaptists mostly lack such embodiment. Our Anabaptist convictions are in danger of being idealized or even ideological, which is partly why we are attempting to plant Anabaptist churches. We have long recognized the importance of building relationships with and learning from historic Mennonite communities in Europe, North America, and elsewhere that have embodied these convictions over many years. But maybe our different context and our more recent discovery of Anabaptism give us fresh insights or even enable us to encourage longstanding Anabaptist communities to engage afresh with the radical Christianity of their spiritual forebears.

My primary misgiving about these four books is that they are largely descriptive of inherited and familiar Mennonite practices that have seemed to be appropriate in a cultural context that retains much more residual Christian influence than emerging Anabaptist communities in the UK experience. Both Roth and Augsburger in different ways challenge their readers to reflect thoughtfully on these practices, to imbue them with deeper significance, and to live out the convictions that undergird them. In his concluding section, entitled "Looking Forward," Roth recognizes "the confusion and anxiety in the church today as it faces an uncertain future,"[16] and encourages fresh thinking about some ecclesial practices. But the four books appear not to recognize how much the society where their Mennonite communities are set is changing, or the speed of these changes. There is little acknowledgment of post-Christendom or postcolonial realities; the cultural components of many of their practices; the declining numbers and limited influence of Mennonite churches in North America; the spirituality of Hispanic, Asian, and African communities in North America; or the shift of ecclesial gravity that means most Anabaptist communities are now in the Majority World. There is little sense of urgency or much awareness that inherited forms of church and traditional approaches to mission are failing to incarnate the good news in a rapidly changing culture. As a snapshot of Anabaptist spirituality and discipleship in traditional North American churches at the start of the twenty-first century, these books are informative and instructive. But they do not break much new ground or ask awkward questions about ecclesial and missional practices—which is the legacy of their troublesome sixteenth-century forebears.

A further misgiving is that all four books were written by middle-aged, tertiary-educated men. There is nothing unusual about this. I fit squarely into that category, as do most authors of Christian books on ecclesiology and missiology. But patriarchy is another malign legacy of post-Christendom, and the domination of male authors on these and other subjects needs to be challenged. Consequently, I have invited three female colleagues to contribute chapters—not only because they are women but because they are pioneering three missional initiatives in Britain and Ireland that are rooted in Anabaptist convictions and represent creative expressions of the common practices that are explored in other chapters.[17]

The domination of White, Western authors in post-Christendom is also problematic, not least because it tends to overlook the growing influence of Christians from the Majority World in Western societies. I have greatly appreciated recent contributions on missiology and ecclesiology from African colleagues who lead mission agencies in the UK (albeit not writing from an Anabaptist perspective).[18] I have also been challenged and inspired by the writings of Black American Anabaptists, including Drew G. I. Hart, an American theologian/activist who calls himself an "Anablacktivist" and integrates Anabaptist and postcolonial perspectives; and Osheta Moore, a pastor in Saint Paul, Minnesota.[19] I am also learning from my interaction with a small network of mostly Zimbabwean Brethren in Christ churches in the UK. They are rediscovering their Anabaptist heritage and exploring the integration of Anabaptist practices and Zimbabwean culture. I have been challenged and inspired by a visit to South Africa and engagement with the Anabaptist Network there, and by supervising South African Anabaptist postgraduate students.[20] And I am privileged to work with African and Caribbean colleagues on the Black Light course, which encourages Christians in the UK from diverse ethnic and cultural backgrounds to grapple with the legacies of Christendom and colonialism.[21]

In the chapters that follow, I will draw on some of these experiences as I explore Anabaptist common practices in this context. There is an integral and mutually reinforcing relationship between Christendom and colonialism, between "Christian supremacy" and White supremacy.[22] This was not something to which *The Naked Anabaptist* gave adequate attention.

IDENTIFYING COMMON PRACTICES

The first six chapters explore twelve practices that neo-Anabaptists in the UK have identified as likely to characterize communities and initiatives that are shaped by the Anabaptist tradition. As acknowledged earlier, these practices have only recently been formulated and are still being explored and assessed.

The process began with a conversation in what was then the steering group of the Anabaptist Network. The term *common practices* was proposed as an indicative but non-prescriptive way to identify practices that seemed to flow naturally out of the core convictions which functioned as the network's center of gravity. A little later, a small group was invited to develop an initial list of such practices in order to stimulate further discussion. This group presented their suggestions at a gathering in March 2020, just before the UK went into lockdown as COVID-19 swept the country. During that weekend, their proposals were tested and debated, some were widely endorsed, others were discarded, and still others were added.

In the following weeks, a revised list was circulated, and further comments were invited. By the summer, there seemed to be widespread endorsement of the twelve practices that we will examine in this book (the full list is spelled out in appendix 2). Later that year, a summary of these practices was disseminated, together with a short study guide, in the hope that individuals and groups would reflect on them and share their responses. Although we have not added to or changed the twelve practices since then, the list remains tentative and open to further development. Consequently, the chapters that follow offer minor revisions of the wording of these practices, examine them in a different order, and explore the links between them. They offer another opportunity to reflect on these practices, and we invite readers to respond and join the conversation.[23]

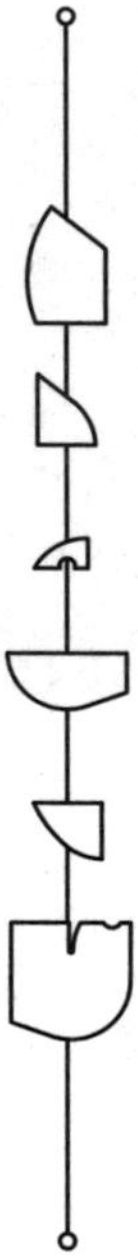

Section I

COMMON PRACTICES

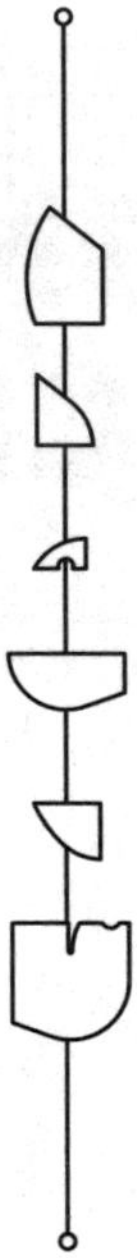

1

STARTING
WITH JESUS

I have often been asked what attracted me to the Anabaptist vision. I can give a number of different answers. Mennonite writings on issues of peace and justice were very significant for me as a young urban church planter in the mid-1980s. Meeting Alan and Eleanor Kreider, directors of the London Mennonite Centre at that time, introduced me to contemporary Anabaptists. Investigating the sixteenth-century Anabaptist movements and their approach to biblical interpretation for a PhD gave me a historical perspective and led me to explore other representatives of what I perceived as a radical tradition within and on the edge of Christendom. This in turn challenged me to wrestle with the implications of the demise of the Christendom era and persuaded me that the Anabaptist vision has much to offer followers of Jesus Christ in post-Christendom societies. In common with several others in Britain and Ireland in the late 1990s, I felt as though I had "come home" when I encountered the Anabaptist tradition.[1]

I could mention other influences and other aspects of Anabaptism that attracted me, but I have often replied that what I am most grateful for is the way Anabaptism has introduced me afresh to the person of Jesus. The Anabaptist vision is profoundly and resolutely Christocentric in ways that I had not previously encountered. I grew up in an evangelical church and became familiar with the story of Jesus at a young age. I am deeply grateful for many features of that upbringing and for those who shared their faith with me. But as I look back, I perceive that little of the preaching and teaching focused on the Gospels or on the life of Jesus. Old Testament texts and the New Testament letters featured strongly. At Christmas and Easter, we heard again the birth narratives and the accounts of the death and resurrection of Jesus. But rarely was there anything on the life of Jesus, his disruptive teaching, miracles, encounters, conflicts with the authorities, friendships, struggles, and example. Just as the creeds move straight from "born of the virgin Mary" to "suffered under Pontius Pilate," there seemed to be little interest in everything that happened in between these events. We heard over and over again why Jesus had to die but nothing about the reasons why he was killed by those who felt threatened by his life and teachings. And on many topics—doctrinal, ethical, and ecclesial—we turned to the Old Testament or to the Epistles (especially Paul's letters) for guidance, rather than to the life and teaching of Jesus.

Maybe I am misremembering, but others who grew up in the evangelical tradition report a similar lacuna. The redeeming work of Jesus was absolutely central—I am not suggesting for a moment that we should underplay this. After all, the gospel writers devote substantial portions of their accounts to his death and resurrection, which is the climax of all four gospels. Furthermore, the true humanity of Jesus was strongly affirmed, alongside his divinity. But his life and teaching seemed to be of little interest or importance. What attracted me to Anabaptism was its insistence that the life and teaching of Jesus are profoundly important, that the gospel stories are not just for children, that there is an organic link between the life that Jesus lived and the death he died, that Jesus is the focal point of the Scriptures, that his teachings are to be lived, not just admired, and that we are called to follow him. The more I embraced this perspective, the more I realized that starting with Jesus makes a real difference in how we understand everything else. And the Anabaptist Mennonite Network has grown as many others have discovered and welcomed this approach.

The first of the common practices that we anticipated would characterize communities inspired by the Anabaptist vision was summarized as "interpreting and following the way of Jesus." And key to this practice is a commitment to starting with Jesus.

NOT A FLAT BIBLE

Starting with Jesus represents a wholehearted rejection of a "flat Bible" approach, in which texts from any part of Scripture are regarded as authoritative without reference to their context or other biblical passages.[2] Starting with Jesus means perceiving the Bible as an unfolding narrative, revealing God's dealings with the nation of ancient Israel, the church, and the whole of humanity. The big story the Bible tells starts with creation and ends with the new creation. Within the Bible are many smaller stories and many different kinds of literature—poetry, history, prophecy, parables, lament, legislation, cautionary tales, genealogies, and much else. But the big story has a center—the life, death, resurrection, and ascension of Jesus. Everything that comes before and after this needs to be interpreted in the light of what Jesus said and did. We need the whole of the Bible to get the full picture. But if Jesus is the supreme revelation of God, we will want to make sure he is at the very center of how we read the Bible. In my teaching, I often refer to the opening verses of the letter to the Hebrews: "Long ago God spoke to our ancestors in many and various ways by the prophets, but in these last days he has spoken to us by a Son" (Hebrews 1:1–2). What God said before is not obsolete, but it needs to be interpreted in light of what God has said definitively through Jesus Christ.

So, neo-Anabaptists choose unapologetically to prioritize the life and teaching of Jesus. We immerse ourselves in the Gospels and commit ourselves to starting with what Jesus said and did in relation to any topic under discussion. We are convinced that this starting point makes a significant difference to how we address questions and understand issues. We believe that starting anywhere else has historically led to the life and teaching of Jesus being marginalized and explained away. Like the early Anabaptists, we are convinced that Jesus is the focal point and primary interpreter of Scripture. We anticipate that a Jesus-centered approach can help us discern and reject the many compromises and distortions of the fast-fading Christendom era and discover ways of following Jesus faithfully in post-Christendom.

Criticisms of this supposedly naïve approach were listed in *The Naked Anabaptist*: It risks downgrading other parts of Scripture and setting up a "canon within the canon." It might imply that the life and teaching of Jesus can be understood without reference to all that led up to this and that his contemporaries did not need this interpretive lens as they reflected on their encounters with Jesus in light of their people's history, hopes, and expectations. Several other books in the New Testament predate the Gospels, giving us additional information about Jesus and various ways of interpreting the significance of his life, death, and resurrection. And more skeptical critics question the reliability of the Gospels as a faithful record of what Jesus did and said, although current biblical scholarship is less dismissive than in a previous generation.[3]

These are serious concerns, and their challenges need to be heeded if we are to avoid unwarranted claims and draw on the resources of the entire biblical library. But in that library we find many different perspectives, emphases, convictions, practices, priorities, behaviors, and theologies. We are drawn into conversations between different eras, different writers, different interpretations of God and history, different ethical prescriptions, and different ways of assessing outcomes. How do we judge between these? Which are authoritative? Whose guidance do we follow? There may be, as some have argued, a trajectory we can follow, even some form of progressive revelation, but there are enough anomalies and uncertainties to trouble us. Allowing the Old Testament to determine our approach to theological, ethical, and ecclesial matters results in ways of thinking and behaving that marginalize what Jesus said and did. This approach undergirded the distortions and inhumanity of Christendom and colonialism. But even if we prioritize the New Testament over the Old, as the early Anabaptists insisted—regarding the Old as preparatory and a mere shadow of what was to come—the New Testament writers do not all seem to speak with one voice on every issue.

The practice we are advocating here is to start with Jesus. What did Jesus say on the issue? What can we learn from his lifestyle, his interactions with others, and his priorities? To interpret the way of Jesus responsibly, we will also need to draw on other parts of Scripture, so arguably we could start anywhere as long as we engage with the life and teaching of Jesus. But in practice, the starting point makes a real difference. Starting elsewhere risks making up our minds before we get to Jesus and then hunting for ways to fit his radical words and enigmatic actions into a framework we have already constructed.

SOME EXAMPLES

It may be helpful to consider some examples—including issues on which the early Anabaptists profoundly disagreed with their contemporaries because of their very different starting points.

Baptism

The early Anabaptists objected to the practice of infant baptism for several reasons: infants could not exercise faith; they were innocent and so not endangered by being unbaptized; baptizing infants who had no choice was an imposition; infant baptism falsely assured people that they were Christians and resulted in low moral standards in the state churches; and this practice was instituted by and supported a false Christendom. But a fundamental objection was that it was inconsistent with the explicit teaching of Jesus and with the record of his life in the Gospels.

Their opponents claimed that infant baptism was justified by an analogy to the Old Testament rite of circumcision. This frustrated the Anabaptists, not least because their opponents seemed to move seamlessly between the Testaments in a way that the Anabaptists regarded as illegitimate. Balthasar Hubmaier complained to Ulrich Zwingli: "For the sake of the last judgment, drop your circuitous argument on circumcision out of the Old Testament. . . . We have a clear word for baptizing believers and you have none for baptizing your children, except that you groundlessly drag in several shadows from the Old Testament."[4]

A gospel text of huge significance to the Anabaptists was "Go therefore and make disciples of all nations, baptizing them in the name of the Father and of the Son and of the Holy Spirit" (Matthew 28:19). Later generations would label this "the great commission" and regard it as the biblical basis for global evangelization. This text inspired some Anabaptist mission activities, but its primary function within their communities was to justify their approach to baptism. The order in this verse was critical—making disciples precedes baptizing. Infants cannot be disciples and so should not be baptized. Baptism is for those who have responded to the gospel and committed themselves to a life of discipleship. This order appears in the other text they frequently quoted: "Go into all the world and proclaim the good news to the whole creation. The one who believes and is baptized will be saved" (Mark 16:15–16).

These are the last recorded words of Jesus in the Gospels and so should be taken with the utmost seriousness and regarded as definitive on the issue of baptism. The narrative leading up to these words offers no reason to question their implications. Jesus welcomed children and blessed them, but did not baptize them. His disciples baptized on Jesus' authority others who wanted to be his disciples (John 4:1–2), as John the Baptist had baptized those who came in repentance (Matthew 3:6). And, of course, Jesus himself had been baptized as an adult (Matthew 3:13).

Those who defend the practice of infant baptism not only continue to use the analogy to circumcision but also point to examples of "household baptisms" (Acts 10:48; 16:33), although these texts do not mention children. A range of theological and pastoral arguments supplement reliance on these rather slim biblical resources. If these arguments are marshaled effectively, and New Testament texts on baptism that make no sense if applied to infants are ignored, advocates of infant baptism can sound persuasive. For hundreds of years this practice undergirded the Christendom system, in which infant baptism represented entrance into a supposedly Christian society. But this marginalized the life and teaching of Jesus. Starting with Jesus does not preclude this interpretation, in that Jesus does not explicitly oppose the baptism of infants, but it makes it much less likely.

War

Three main perspectives on the issue of warfare are evident throughout church history: just war, holy war or crusade, and pacifism.

- The dominant position for many centuries in the European churches was the doctrine of just war, which set out criteria to assess the legitimacy and mode of conduct of warfare. Its origins were in classical philosophy, but it had been given a theological makeover by the theologian Augustine to provide ethical guidance for an emerging "Christian" empire. Augustine struggled to find much biblical support for this, but it seemed to offer a realistic approach throughout the Christendom era, when warfare was rife and "Christian" nations had borders to defend. This remains the dominant view, although it is facing increasing scrutiny in light of the realities of modern warfare, where the criteria are very difficult to apply.
- Far more biblical support, although primarily from the Old Testament, could be found for holy war, when the restrictions of the just war doctrine could be set aside as Christian warriors fought to annihilate infidels and establish or expand the reach of Christendom.

Many texts could be quoted to justify holy war, even if closer examination suggests rather more nuanced inter-pretations might be appropriate.

- Pacifism—the renunciation of lethal violence—was the dominant approach in the early churches, but during the Christendom era it was advocated only by dissident movements and a handful of mainstream church leaders. Those like the Anabaptists who promoted and practiced pacifism did so on the basis of the life and teachings of Jesus. This was deeply threatening to church and society and provoked persecution.

Advocates of infant baptism have needed to draw on other biblical passages in the absence of any support from the Gos-pels, but those who reject pacifism can argue their case on the basis of what Jesus did and said. There are texts in the Gospels that might seem to undermine the pacifist position. These include the account of Jesus driving the traders out of the temple courts (Matthew 21:12) and his enigmatic instruc-tion to the disciples that "the one who has no sword must sell his cloak and buy one" (Luke 22:36). Jesus' interaction with a Roman centurion (Matthew 8:5–13) contains no hint of criti-cism of the man's occupation, nor do John the Baptist's words to soldiers who came for baptism (Luke 3:14). Starting with Jesus on this issue does not provide univocal testimony—a warning to advocates of this approach that it does not resolve everything as neatly as we might wish.

Since in every other way the life and teachings of Jesus point us toward a life of nonviolence, reconciliation, and active peacemaking, those who advocate the legitimacy of followers of Jesus Christ participating actively in warfare primarily use these texts to undermine this conclusion. However, these texts

that supposedly undermine the pacifist position can be interpreted in other ways and, individually and together, offer a
rather shaky foundation for adopting any doctrine or philosophy of warfare. Not surprisingly, then, critics of pacifism place
much greater reliance on other biblical texts, especially in the
Old Testament but also in the book of Revelation. Some suggest that Jesus is portrayed in Revelation as a violent warrior,
despite numerous indications in the text that this is misguided.
I recall an influential church leader at a conference several
years ago proclaiming that "Jesus in the Gospels may have
advocated turning the other cheek, but Revelation shows us
what he is really like!" Actually, this extraordinary book *does*
show us what Jesus is like if we pay attention to its subversive
imagery, such as where the seer expected a lion but discovered
a lamb (Revelation 5:5–6).[5]

Starting with Jesus as we reflect on issues of violence and
war requires us to listen carefully to his teachings as he blesses
the peacemakers, urges creative nonviolent responses to oppression, rejects provocations to violence, submits to injustice
and state-sponsored violence, invites his disciples to speak
peace to those they visit, asks God to forgive his persecutors,
yearns for Jerusalem to experience peace, and prays peace upon
his frightened followers after his resurrection. Starting with
Jesus might also mean reflecting on the prominence of peace
in the nativity narratives and their prophetic foreshadowing
(Isaiah 9:6–7; Micah 5:2–5; Luke 1:76–79; 2:13–14). And
starting with Jesus might mean prioritizing ways of becoming
peacemakers and peace advocates in local and global contexts.

Oaths

The early Anabaptists lived in a society where swearing
oaths was far more important than it is in ours—although

oaths are still used in a surprising number of contexts today. But in the sixteenth century, oaths were meant to guarantee honesty in business transactions, telling the truth in court, civic loyalty, and readiness to defend one's homeland or go to war. The steadfast refusal of most (though not all) Anabaptists to swear oaths was another reason why they were regarded as a danger to society, which would, according to some of their contemporaries, descend into chaos if oaths were not sworn.

Anabaptists offered various reasons for not swearing oaths, including concern that doing so was presumptuous in that they could not guarantee future outcomes, and reluctance to embrace a system that implied truth-telling mattered only when oaths had been sworn. But their main reason was fidelity to the explicit teaching of Jesus in the Sermon on the Mount: "Do not swear at all, either by heaven, for it is the throne of God, or by the earth, for it is his footstool, or by Jerusalem, for it is the city of the great King. And do not swear by your head, for you cannot make one hair white or black. Let your word be 'Yes, Yes' or 'No, No'; anything more than this comes from the evil one" (Matthew 5:34–37). This teaching is clear, categorical, and without exception, so it may seem surprising that some Anabaptists and almost all their contemporaries continued to swear oaths and defend this practice.

But the Old Testament includes over a hundred instances of oaths being sworn. Indeed, Jesus refers to these before forbidding his disciples to swear oaths: "You have heard that it was said to those of ancient times, 'You shall not swear falsely, but carry out the vows you have made to the Lord'" (Matthew 5:33). There is no indication in these Old Testament texts that swearing oaths was wrong. What mattered was keeping oaths or vows. Furthermore, there are examples of God swearing oaths! And in the New Testament, texts refer to Paul taking a vow (Acts 18:18) or calling on God as witness to what he is writing (Romans 1:9; 2 Corinthians 1:23; Galatians 1:20; Philippians 1:8); several references in Hebrews are uncritical of swearing oaths (e.g., 6:16); and even an angel swears an oath (Revelation 10:6). The only explicit reference to Jesus' teaching on this subject is James 5:12, which repeats it almost word for word.

As with other topics where biblical texts seem to point in different directions, it is possible to offer interpretations that harmonize them: calling God to witness is not the same as swearing an oath; vows and promises are voluntary and do not imply divine sanction if they are broken; God alone can swear an oath because only God can guarantee not breaking it; swearing oaths in the Old Testament was appropriate then but is not now; and so on. We may need to choose. Does the explicit teaching of Jesus outweigh the other texts, or do these relativize his teaching? Do we start with Jesus and consider the other texts in light of his words, or do we start elsewhere and try to fit his uncompromising teaching into what we have discovered elsewhere? The uncertainty among the early Anabaptists suggests they struggled to know what to do, although over time refusal to swear oaths became normative.

Tithing

The Christendom system was expensive. A massive church bureaucracy, extravagant buildings, and thousands of clergy required financial support on a huge scale. Voluntary contributions never would have sufficed, but the introduction of compulsory tithing and its ruthless administration enabled the state churches to become extremely wealthy. Limited provision for the poor from the tithes in no way offset the injustice of the system and the hardship it caused. Tithe resistance was frequent. This was one of the grievances that provoked the so-called Peasants' War in the mid-1520s, in which many of the early Anabaptists were involved. This plea for social and economic reform was harshly suppressed.[6] After all, tithing had plenty of biblical support, it was argued.

Tithing today is entirely voluntary, although psychological pressure in some churches can be quite daunting, but tithing is remarkably popular in some traditions. Ignorance of the immense suffering caused by this regressive church tax may be partly to blame for the survival of this approach to economic discipleship, but failing to start with Jesus in relation to this issue results in churches advocating a practice that is "biblical" but not Christian.[7]

Jesus often spoke about economic issues—social justice, wealth and poverty, giving and sharing. What he said is challenging but also liberating, as he invites us to free ourselves from the domination of Mammon. But he never taught his disciples to tithe. The only references to tithing in the Gospels are comments on the legalistic and self-justifying practices of the Pharisees. Starting with Jesus not only offers no biblical basis for tithing but suggests it is an inappropriate practice for his followers. Nor is there any encouragement to tithe in the rest of the New Testament. Pleas to support mission activities, Christian workers, and poor fellow-Christians are not buttressed by appeals to tithing. Quite different, and more radical, principles and practices are invoked. Nor is there any evidence that tithing was advocated or practiced in the early churches, which engaged different and more radical economic practices and criticized tithing as unsuitable for Christians.

Tithing was an Old Testament practice, although precisely how it operated is by no means clear. It was one component in a complex economic system that involved the remission of debt, freewill offerings, gleaning, hospitality, sabbath years, and much else, at the heart of which was the proclamation of jubilee. Every fifty years, Israel was to experience a social and economic upheaval that would diminish inequality and offer a new start to those who had been struggling. Leviticus 25 sets out what was required. While there is no evidence that jubilee was ever fully implemented, aspects of this legislation were, and it remained a prophetic hope ("the year of the LORD's favor" in Isaiah 61:2).

Although not all are persuaded, many biblical scholars have concluded that Jesus embraced this vision of jubilee when he read Isaiah's prophecy in the synagogue at Nazareth and declared: "Today this scripture has been fulfilled in your hearing" (Luke 4:21). "Forgive us our debts, as we also have forgiven our debtors" in the Lord's Prayer (Matthew 6:12) also has a strong resonance with the language of jubilee. Indeed, some suggest that the language of jubilee permeates the teaching of Jesus and that the sharing of possessions by the church in Jerusalem, which resulted in there being "not a needy person among them" (Acts 4:34), was inspired by a vision of jubilee.

Starting with the Old Testament references to tithing, especially when there is no recognition of the wider economic context, has led many to assume this provides a mandate for followers of Jesus. The most that can then be said in relation to Jesus is that he nowhere forbade tithing and in one place urged the Pharisees who practiced this to set it in a context of "justice and mercy and faith" (Matthew 23:23). But if we start with Jesus, we are almost overwhelmed by the extent and exciting radicality of his economic teachings, in light of which the practice of tithing, extracted from its jubilee context, not only has little to offer but actually hinders engagement with what Jesus taught.

Women in leadership

In early Anabaptist communities, women actively participated much more than in the state churches. They were encouraged to use their gifts and contribute to discussions about biblical interpretation, and they sometimes exercised leadership roles. While there is little discussion of the role of women in early Anabaptist writings, the practice of the churches indicates that they regarded such participation as consistent with Scripture.[8]

Those who believe that leadership in the church (and often in the home, if not in all spheres of life) should be restricted to men may seek support for this position from the gospel narratives that indicate Jesus chose twelve men to be apostles but no women. However, this position is more firmly established by those passages in the Epistles that seem to place significant limitations on women (especially 1 Corinthians 14:34 and 1 Timothy 2:11–12). These passages, of course, are open to interpretation, and other passages appear to assume that women are exercising significant leadership roles, not least those where Paul greets female colleagues (e.g., Romans 16:1, 7, 12; Colossians 4:15). As in the Old Testament, a male-dominated narrative is shot through with examples of women exercising significant leadership roles. And the clarion statement "There is no longer Jew or Greek, there is no longer slave or free, there is no longer male and female; for all of you are one in Christ Jesus" (Galatians 3:28) is liberating, rather than restrictive.

Readers confronted with a range of texts, some of them apparently restrictive, others seemingly liberative, may be tempted either to conclude that there is no authoritative position on this issue or to choose the position with which they are personally most comfortable. Others may argue that despite the diversity of the texts, there is a clear trajectory—albeit not a uniform one—that leads toward a liberative position. In practice, our engagement with this issue is a good example of how much depends on our starting point and whether we read the Bible as a flat book.

Starting with Jesus encourages us to immerse ourselves in gospel narratives that include numerous encounters between Jesus and women (especially in Luke). How Jesus speaks to and about women, includes them in his company and his teaching, rejects patriarchal and misogynistic stereotyping, and invites them to be his disciples may not provide conclusive support for women in church leadership, but should at least affect our assumptions and the tone of any discussion of this issue.

NO PANACEA BUT AN OPPORTUNITY

But what about issues on which Jesus said nothing, according to the gospel writers, but which are addressed in other biblical passages? Do we assume that Jesus had no view on these matters? Or that he accepted what Old Testament texts taught or what his contemporaries believed? Some of the most contentious ethical debates in recent years have concerned issues of human sexuality. The growing acceptance, indeed advocacy and celebration, of diverse sexual activities and relationships in Western societies (but not in much of the Majority World) has provoked many followers of Jesus to reassess relevant biblical texts but has convinced others that they need to resist this cultural shift. Although not many texts on this subject appear in either Testament, those that do seem, at least on the surface, to be uniformly opposed to sexual activity between same-sex partners, despite various efforts to interpret them differently or to differentiate contemporary practices from those the biblical texts were seemingly addressing.

But there is no record of Jesus addressing this issue, so what might it mean to start with Jesus in this context? We might assume that Jesus accepted without question or need to state his view on the traditional Jewish opposition to same-sex practices. We might conclude that terms used by Jesus to condemn sexual immorality (such as *porneia* and *aselgeia*) would have been understood by his hearers to include same-sex relationships. We might start with what Jesus taught about marriage and his apparent assumption that this involved a man and a woman. However, we might also wonder about Jesus' encounter with a caring Roman centurion (Matthew 8:5–13), who pleaded for healing for his male servant in such passionate language that some have suggested that a sexual relationship may have been involved (which would not have been unusual in this context). Jesus not only healed the servant but commended the centurion's exemplary faith. Or we might interpret Jesus' apparent silence on this issue, especially compared with what he taught so clearly about nonviolence or economic discipleship, as implicitly distancing himself from Jewish hostility to same-sex practice or at least constituting a rebuke to those for whom this is a line-in-the-sand issue and worth dividing over. And what Jesus says about loving our enemies might be of great relevance in contexts where strong disagreements over belief and practice threaten to damage our relationships and cause great pain.

And there are issues on which Jesus was quite clear but his disciples offered a less demanding perspective. An example is the issue of divorce, on which it seems that Jesus adopted a rigorous position in his teaching and in his exchanges with the Pharisees: "Anyone who divorces his wife, except on the ground of unchastity, causes her to commit adultery; and whoever marries a divorced woman commits adultery" (Matthew 5:32;

see also 19:1–9). Mark and Luke are even stronger, omitting the exception clause. But Paul, in an extended discussion about mixed marriages between a believer and a nonbeliever, seems to offer more nuanced pastoral guidance, allowing for divorce in marriages without peace and indicating that this was his position, rather than that of Jesus (1 Corinthians 7:1–16). Starting with Jesus, it seems, does not preclude further reflection and pastoral sensitivity.

These different examples indicate that starting with Jesus is no panacea. It does not resolve every issue or offer guidance on every subject. But a commitment to starting with Jesus invites us to investigate his life and teaching thoroughly, rather than assuming that on some topics the Gospels have nothing to offer, or turning too quickly to other biblical texts. And while the rest of the Bible helps us understand the life and teaching of Jesus, starting with Jesus provides the interpretive framework for everything else.

Those who are familiar with European church history will recognize that, for most of the issues we have considered, there is a significant mismatch between the beliefs and practices of the early churches and those of churches in the Christendom era. The early Christians did not baptize infants, except occasionally for pastoral reasons. Most refused to participate in warfare or to defend themselves violently. There is no evidence that tithing was practiced, despite much teaching on lifestyle, generosity, and the dangers of wealth. And, although patriarchy reasserted itself, many women exercised significant leadership roles in the churches. But in the Christendom era, the radical teachings of Jesus were marginalized in favor of biblical texts that were more congenial to a nominally Christian empire. Christendom practices may have been biblical, but many of them were not Christian.

Perhaps the transition to a post-Christendom culture in most Western societies gives us an opportunity to reconsider the witness of the early churches, to learn from the Jesus-centered instincts of the Anabaptists and other dissenting movements through the centuries, and to recover an approach to biblical interpretation—and practical application—that starts with Jesus and takes his life and teaching with the utmost seriousness. If "starting with Jesus" is not only an interpretive strategy but a serious commitment to following Jesus as his disciples, neo-Anabaptist communities may be well placed to seize this opportunity and test out its implications. But we do well to bear in mind both parts of a well-known early Anabaptist statement. "No one can know Christ unless he follows after him in life," wrote German Anabaptist leader Hans Denck. But he continued: "and no one can follow him unless he first knows him."[9]

Starting with and following Jesus must not reduce discipleship to ethics or Jesus to a great teacher or wonderful example. Nor should a renewed focus on the significance of his life and teaching tempt us in any way to minimize the salvific significance of his death, resurrection, ascension, and gift of the Holy Spirit. Starting with Jesus means both rejoicing in the salvation he achieved for us and gratefully learning to both know and follow him. As the first of the Anabaptist Mennonite Network's core convictions states (see appendix 1), Jesus is our redeemer and Lord, as well as our example and teacher, and the source of our life.

Emerging Anabaptist communities will be committed to following Jesus, but we will also seek the help of the Holy Spirit, whom Jesus promised would teach, guide, and empower his disciples.

Explaining to them that "I still have many things to say to you, but you cannot bear them now," Jesus promised that "when the Spirit of truth comes, he will guide you into all the truth" (John 16:12–13). If we understand this as an invitation to explore issues on which Jesus was silent, we will do so with two crucial caveats. First, we will be wary of confusing the voice of the Holy Spirit with the assumptions and assertions of contemporary culture. And second, we will heed what Jesus also said to his disciples: that the Spirit will "remind you of all that I have said to you" (John 14:26), that the Spirit "will not speak on his own, but will speak whatever he hears," and "will take what is mine and declare it to you" (John 16:13-14). The Spirit also, it seems, starts with Jesus.

2

BAPTISM AND COMMUNION

Baptism and communion are examples of practices that are common in most, though not all, Christian communities. Churches shaped by the Anabaptist tradition practice both and have learned much from the theology and experiences of other traditions, but are likely to bring to them distinctive emphases and perspectives. Common practices of emerging Anabaptist communities, we suggest, are likely to include baptizing would-be disciples and communion as a peace meal.

BAPTISM

As noted, not all branches of the Christian community practice water baptism. The Salvation Army and the Quakers are among those that choose not to do so. But baptism is a very important feature of most Christian denominations. Some regard this practice as a sacrament; others prefer the language of ordinance; for many others it is simply a biblical requirement. Some baptize by full immersion; others by sprinkling or pouring water. Some baptize infants; others baptize young people when they are old enough to consent; others baptize only adults. Some baptize only after a period of instruction;

others on profession of faith. Baptisms may take place in rivers, lakes, the sea, swimming pools, purpose-built baptisteries, or elsewhere. In some traditions, anyone can perform a baptism; in others, this is restricted to ordained ministers or church leaders. Baptism in water may or may not be conjoined in theory or in practice with baptism in the Spirit. Some early Anabaptists added the "baptism of blood," referring both to the cost of serious discipleship and to the suffering that would likely be involved in a society that was outraged by their practice of baptizing as believers those who had been baptized as infants. Those who executed them by drowning sometimes mockingly called this a third baptism.

Church history offers many perspectives on baptism, and these have led to theological arguments, painful divisions, mutual excommunication, and sometimes persecution. As the name imposed on them by their opponents testifies, Anabaptists ("re-baptizers") fell foul of the authorities for their baptismal beliefs and practices. In the previous chapter we noted the reasons for their opposition to infant baptism. But their insistence on baptizing those who had been baptized as infants—on the basis that infant baptism was illegitimate and so this was not rebaptism—was a primary reason why they were arrested, imprisoned, tortured, exiled, or executed. Their refusal to allow their children to be baptized threatened the unity of a sacral society where this rite of passage signified entrance into that society. However much they disagreed with each other on other matters, Catholics and Protestants in the sixteenth century agreed that this disruptive practice could not be tolerated.

It is not easy in our very different context to relate to this level of antipathy over an ecclesial practice. This is not only because of advances in ecumenical relationships, albeit often at the expense of agreeing to ambiguous statements about baptism, but because in a post-Christendom society, a diminishing number of people are being baptized at any age and in any mode. And a commitment to religious liberty or to its rather ambivalent secular equivalent of tolerance precludes anything more than academic arguments and hurt feelings when disagreements over baptism arise.

What then, if anything, might be distinctive about the practice of baptism in neo-Anabaptist communities? Is there an expectation, or requirement, that those who want to join these communities be baptized as believers if they have not already been? What about those who were baptized as infants and may have subsequently been confirmed as an expression of faith and commitment to discipleship? To what extent can such communities claim to be Anabaptist if on these matters they adopt different policies than those who suffered so painfully for their convictions in the sixteenth century? Or is our post-Christendom context sufficiently different that we should respond in other ways? After all, infant baptism was almost ubiquitous and meant entrance into a sacral society in the sixteenth century, but this is certainly not so today. These are issues with which neo-Anabaptist churches and communities will need to wrestle—and in different social contexts may reach different conclusions.

An Anabaptist-Anglican friend, whose pastoral ministry was spent in poor urban neighborhoods, used to insist that infant baptism today is often (though admittedly not always) an expression of countercultural discipleship and, as such, should be encouraged. He was also unwilling to turn away parents asking him to baptize their children, knowing that these parents frequently experienced rebuffs from institutions of all kinds. A very different perspective was presented to me some years ago by a former Anglican priest who asked me whether members of the Anabaptist Network would join him in public protests outside churches that were baptizing infants. He was convinced that this practice was spiritually damaging, deluding those who had been baptized as infants into thinking they were Christians and threatening their eternal destiny. While I recognized in him a passion similar to that of many of the early Anabaptists, much to his disappointment I declined to get involved in what seemed to me an inappropriate way to conduct a theological debate.

Whichever of these very different approaches we find more persuasive, some of the distinctive implications of baptism in the early years of the Anabaptist movement remain highly relevant in our communities, even in our greatly changed cultural context. "Baptism," as I wrote in *The Naked Anabaptist*, "is not only a visible expression of personal faith but a pledge of discipleship, an invitation to mutual accountability, and commitment to active participation in the church community."[1]

A pledge of discipleship

Since receiving believers baptism meant that persecution was likely and execution possible, this was not something to be undertaken lightly. Many more people were attracted to the early Anabaptist communities than were prepared to identify publicly with them in this way. Baptism today might be a courageous act of personal testimony to family, friends, and neighbors, but it does not usually carry such risks in Western societies. In many churches that practice "believers baptism," the person performing the baptism uses the phrase "On your profession of faith, I baptize you." This phrase helpfully places the emphasis on the belief and initiative of the person being baptized, who has responded to the gospel and expressed faith in Jesus Christ, rather than on the institution or the person baptizing. However, perhaps a stronger profession is needed to convey the radical implications of baptism. Indeed, maybe the "baptism of disciples" is more appropriate than the "baptism of believers."

Baptism is both the culmination of a journey of discovery and a staging post on the road of discipleship. Although it is very common to do so, it is not particularly helpful to refer to the first part of the journey as a response to evangelism and the next part as being committed to discipleship, not least because in the Anabaptist tradition, signs of repentance and lifestyle changes have been expected prior to baptism. And the experience of many churches in post-Christendom is that believing, behaving, and belonging may not always happen in the same order. Indeed, some measure of belonging frequently precedes both believing and behaving. But baptism represents a point on the journey when a would-be disciple makes a public pledge, not only of faith in Jesus Christ but of loyalty to his kingdom and readiness to follow wherever he leads.

What about the role of catechesis? In the New Testament it seems that people were baptized as soon as they responded to the gospel, but in the early church era there was usually a lengthy and demanding period of teaching, mentoring, and evaluation (known as catechesis) before people were baptized. Was this because the church was now operating in an environment where those who responded to the gospel did not have the theological, historical, and ethical foundations that Jewish converts would have had, and so more teaching and cultural detoxification was required? If so, it is not surprising that there is growing interest in catechesis in post-Christendom societies. But is there a danger that this delays baptism, a rite of initiation, too long? The text that Anabaptists quoted so frequently on the subject of baptism (Matthew 28:19–20) speaks of baptizing and teaching in that order. Maybe catechesis should mostly follow baptism? Or, if we regard the whole journey as one of discipleship, some form of catechesis (formal or informal) might both precede and follow baptism. However we practice this, catechesis points us toward the role of the community in helping us grow as disciples.

An invitation to mutual accountability

Although baptism represents a personal step of faith, testimony, and commitment to discipleship, in the Anabaptist tradition this is set within a communal framework. The journey of discipleship is taken in the company of others and involves accountability, alongside support and encouragement. This does not erode personal responsibility for living faithfully and drawing on the grace of God, but it acknowledges the reality of temptation and struggle, and makes available the resources of the community. The foundational biblical passage for this practice (although there are many other texts in the New Testament) is Matthew 18:15–20, which early Anabaptists called "the rule of Christ." Referring to this text in *A Christian Instruction*, Balthasar Hubmaier declared that this was a crucial component in "the proper baptismal vow which was lost for the space of a thousand years."[2] Recovering this aspect of discipleship and church life was something the Anabaptists regarded as essential.

We will explore this practice further in another chapter, but note here two crucial aspects. First, the accountability is mutual and involves willingness to both give and receive support, excluding heavy-handed pastoral interventions and inviting all members to "watch over" one another. Author Palmer Becker reports in relation to North American Mennonite churches that "today when new believers desire to join an Anabaptist congregation, they are typically asked, 'Are you willing to give and receive counsel?'"[3] Second, the accountability is entered into voluntarily at the point of baptism, when entry into the church is also celebrated. Those who make this commitment embrace this understanding of community, rather than encountering this practice later and unexpectedly. Planting new Anabaptist churches, then, offers opportunities to embed this aspect of baptism into our ecclesial practice.

This kind of accountability is countercultural in societies that valorize individualism and tolerance. However gentle and gracious interventions of this kind might be, many will balk at the suggestion that others might question our behavior, lifestyle choices, priorities, or relationships—and at the suggestion that we might have a responsibility to confront others. But there are also signs that a younger generation yearns for deeper experiences of community, so mutually accountable friendships may not be as unattractive as we might think. They might even have missional potency, offering an alternative to individualism and lack of authentic community. In any case, in post-Christendom cultures that powerfully and insidiously espouse values and advocate practices that are incompatible with faithful discipleship, we need each other if we are to discern and resist this influence. Actually, in any culture or era, we need each other. The New Testament letters are full of "one another" language.[4] The journey of discipleship is not meant to be an isolated pilgrimage.

Commitment to active participation

Mutual accountability is only one aspect of the commitment those being baptized make to the community. The absence of this commitment within the state churches disqualified these churches in the eyes of the early Anabaptists from being true Christian communities. But they regarded as equally problematic the mono-voiced clericalism in the state churches that resulted in congregations being passive and dependent. In an anonymous tract that gives various reasons why the Anabaptists refused to attend the state churches and planted their own churches, the first reason is that those churches were ignoring Paul's teaching in 1 Corinthians 14 that everyone should be open to the Holy Spirit and be ready to contribute.[5] Relying on one priest or preacher disenfranchised the congregation and quenched the Spirit. The absence of mutual accountability appears only as the fifth reason, and baptizing infants as the seventh: this tract accords a striking priority to openness to the Spirit and active participation in the community.

Again, we will explore this practice further in a later chapter, but note here that those who came forward for baptism were aware that such participation was not only allowed but expected. Anabaptists may have met in secret to avoid discovery and persecution, but their neighbors and opponents knew what kind of churches they were forming. It was evident from their conversations, their missional activities, and their responses under interrogation that they were far from passive. They were equipped and empowered by their active participation in worship, biblical study, and mutual accountability. Baptism into such a community was a commitment to take part as the Spirit led. One of the malign legacies of the Christendom era, when church attendance was compulsory (if not consistently enforced), is passivity. And passivity in congregational gatherings usually results in passivity in witness. But this is not the kind of Christian community we find in the New Testament or in the early years until clericalism and nominal Christianity silenced and disempowered it. And it is not the kind of community that will be attractive or effective in post-Christendom, a culture that is averse to unchallengeable monologues.

Within Anabaptist communities today, then, the baptizing of believers/disciples will be a common practice, even if there is some flexibility in relation to those who were baptized as infants. And this practice will likely include expectations of participation in the life and witness of the community; a commitment to give and receive support, encouragement, and admonition within a framework of mutual accountability; and access to resources, before or after baptism, to nurture faithful discipleship. If these communities are to remain healthy, they will also emphasize "baptism in the Spirit," as the early Anabaptists did. This expression is interpreted in various ways today, but at heart it is about openness to the Spirit's guidance, power, and joy. In light of the tendency within the Anabaptist tradition to focus on ethics at the expense of spirituality, neo-Anabaptist communities will find this a helpful counterbalance.

It is less obvious how the third form of baptism associated with the early Anabaptists, the "baptism in blood," relates to Christian communities in societies where, as Alan Kreider once commented, we are more likely to be "suffocated by tolerance" than to experience active persecution. But maybe, at least, our communities need to remain aware of their participation in a global church where persecution is the experience of many. And, as the phrase was used by early Anabaptists to also refer to the cost of faithful discipleship, regardless of persecution, this rather threatening image might not be entirely irrelevant in communities committed to serious discipleship.

COMMUNION

My friend Noel Moules, who was the originator of the term *the naked Anabaptist*, has also coined an evocative term for what is variously referred to as communion, the eucharist, mass, or the Lord's Supper. He calls it "the peacemeal."[6] This term points us toward emphases and practices that are likely to characterize emerging Anabaptist communities.

In 1 Corinthians 11:20–34, Paul gives instructions about how the church is to remember Jesus in the context of a meal, recalling for his readers the occasion when Jesus had shared a final supper with his disciples. The middle section of this passage (vv. 23–26), which reports the actions and words of Jesus, is familiar, and is frequently read in preparation for sharing bread and wine together. Much less often are the verses preceding and after this included, where Paul challenges the behavior of the Corinthians, even though these verses are intimately connected and provide the context for Paul's teaching on the practice of communion. Paul is very concerned about division and injustice, which makes a mockery of communion and invites judgment on the church.

In many churches, including the one in which I grew up, the historical and vertical aspects of communion are central—looking back to the death of Jesus and up to the God who has reconciled us through the death of Jesus. But the verses before and after the central passage invite the Corinthians (and us) to be equally aware of the present and horizontal aspects of sharing bread and wine together. And peace is at the heart of this practice.

Sharing bread and wine is an opportunity to remember the peacemaking work of Jesus, described in Ephesians 2:14–18:

> For he is our peace; in his flesh he has made both groups into one and has broken down the dividing wall, that is, the hostility between us. He has abolished the law with its commandments and ordinances, so that he might create in

himself one new humanity in place of the two, thus making peace, and might reconcile both groups to God in one body through the cross, thus putting to death that hostility through it. So he came and proclaimed peace to you who were far off and peace to those who were near; for through him both of us have access in one Spirit to the Father.

At the heart of communion is an extraordinary act of peacemaking, although what we look back to is actually a moment of injustice and extreme violence. Jesus was crucified—rejected and framed by the religious leaders of his own people and then executed at the whim of the occupying army. When we dig deeper into the story, we find ourselves there, complicit in this act of violence. When God walked the earth and demonstrated what it means to be truly human, our guilty consciences could not cope, and we had to destroy him. Jesus called us to love our enemies, but we made him our enemy and killed him. Dig even deeper into the story and we find what Aslan in C. S. Lewis's fictional world of Narnia would call the "deep magic."[7] Through the death of Jesus, God was making peace, forgiving sins, reconciling enemies, and restoring relationships. Rather than destroying those who had made themselves his enemies, repaying violence with violence, God in Christ absorbed the violence and hostility, breaking the vicious circle and making peace possible.

Communion is an invitation to remember the peacemaking work of Jesus, through which we are not only reconciled to God but also to each other across all that would divide us. At this shared meal we can reaffirm our commitment to each other and to a peaceful community. Injustice and division within the community that shares bread and wine inevitably contradict the essential meaning of the Lord's Supper. But if

1 Corinthians 11:20–22 and 27–34 are excluded or ignored, we can fail to grapple with this challenge.

In addition to the tendency in many churches to focus almost exclusively on the vertical aspect of communion, two other features of contemporary practice discourage the recovery of communion as a "peace meal." The first is the tendency to individualize the act of eating bread and drinking wine. In some churches, this is symbolized and expressed by the use of tiny individual cups and accompanied by an ethos where each gives thanks in silence. The instruction to "all drink together" from these cups to express unity is little compensation. This is often defended on health grounds in order to avoid passing on infections, not least in light of the COVID-19 pandemic, and to protect those who are immunocompromised. These are valid concerns, which will require communities to be both creative and responsible. In other churches, priests or ministers dispense tiny pieces of bread or wafers to individuals kneeling in front of them.

The second feature is the removal of communion from the context of a real meal. Communion was originally celebrated in the context of real meals—not just at the Last Supper but in the early churches (as was obviously the practice in Corinth) and for many decades after. Eating together and sharing bread and wine as part of a meal provides a much better context for communion as a "peace meal." Eating together gives us an opportunity to confront relational issues, rather than pretending we are at peace or avoiding those who are different from us or with whom we are in conflict. This does not, of course, guarantee right relationships or unity, as is evident from what Paul writes to the Corinthians, but it does bring problems into the light. In Corinth, social and economic divisions were damaging the community. They were not acting justly or caring for each other. The church was not at peace. Indeed, because of this Paul insists that they were not actually eating the Lord's Supper at all (v. 20). But because communion was celebrated in the context of a real meal, the divisions had become visible, and this issue could be addressed.

When and why did communion become detached from a real meal? Perhaps not surprisingly, this practice fell into disrepute during the fourth century. The Christendom shift that resulted from the emperor Constantine's decision to embrace Christianity exacerbated an ongoing move toward clericalism and formalism. Communion was now celebrated in institutional settings, rather than a communal context, and the distribution of bread and wine to the congregation was restricted to the clergy. The earlier unregulated, multivoiced love feasts, where food was shared, conversations were enjoyed, and community was built, could no longer be tolerated. These were potentially disruptive of clerical control. In 397, the Council of Carthage finally forbade them.

Some churches have a practice known as "passing the peace," when members greet each other with the words "Peace be with you!" If this practice is taken seriously, it is an opportunity to resolve conflict, bless each other, and prepare to share bread and wine together with integrity. Other communities, especially those that celebrate communion infrequently, set aside time for preparation and encourage members to be reconciled to each other before sharing bread and wine. Some of the historic peace churches incorporate footwashing into their communion services—a very physical expression of loving service and being at peace with one another.[8] These practices can help ensure that communion is indeed a "peace meal." But it may well be that a real meal remains the most appropriate context.

Eating together plays a central role in the Gospels. Jesus was frequently at table. The four Gospels contain twenty-eight references to Jesus eating and drinking with others; even considering parallel passages, these include at least seventeen separate occasions.[9] Jesus often drew on the imagery of meals, wedding feasts, and banquets to illustrate the nature of God's kingdom. He was so often at table that he was even accused of being a drunkard and a glutton (Matthew 11:19)! Eating together symbolizes and expresses acceptance, welcome, inclusion, and hospitality. Who is welcome at our table, and who is not? Several New Testament meals were boundary-breaking, reconciling unlikely people: Zacchaeus, the woman in the house of Simon the Pharisee, Peter in the house of Cornelius. These are all "peace meals" in the broadest sense. Sharing bread and wine in these contexts, in memory of the peacemaking work of Jesus, seems entirely appropriate.

Meals together, especially meals that include communion, look forward to the great banquet at the end of the age—a frequent image in both Testaments:

> On this mountain the LORD of hosts will make for all peoples
>   a feast of rich food, a feast of well-aged wines,
>   of rich food filled with marrow, of well-aged wines
>   strained clear.
> And he will destroy on this mountain
>   the shroud that is cast over all peoples,
>   the sheet that is spread over all nations;
>   he will swallow up death forever. (Isaiah 25:6–8a)

> Then people will come from east and west, from north and south, and will eat in the kingdom of God. Indeed, some are last who will be first, and some are first who will be last. (Luke 13:29–30)

Then I heard what seemed to be the voice of a great multitude, like the sound of many waters and like the sound of mighty thunder peals, crying out,

> "Hallelujah!
> For the Lord our God
>   the Almighty reigns.
> Let us rejoice and exult
>   and give him the glory,
> for the marriage of the Lamb has come,
>   and his bride has made herself ready;
> to her it has been granted to be clothed
>   with fine linen, bright and pure"—

for the fine linen is the righteous deeds of the saints. And the angel said to me, 'Write this: Blessed are those who are invited to the marriage supper of the Lamb.'" (Revelation 19:6–9)

In these and many similar passages, reconciliation and peacemaking are connected with eating together. When we eat together, we are anticipating the great feast when all enemies will be reconciled, all violence ended, and all conflict resolved. When we share bread and wine, we are looking in several directions. We look *back* to God's amazing act of peacemaking. We look *up* to God as reconciled human beings. We look *forward* to the great banquet when all will be reconciled. We look *around* at our diverse table companions and commit ourselves afresh to be at peace. And we look *out* onto a warring world and commit ourselves afresh to be peacemakers.[10]

A common practice, then, in contemporary Anabaptist churches will be communion celebrated in ways that embody and communicate welcome, reconciliation, justice, and peace. Most likely, communion will often be set in the context of shared meals. Some will explore the dynamics of footwashing or introduce contextually appropriate practices that convey a similar meaning. Others might experiment with different kinds of communion—some that are specifically for committed members of the community, others that are missional, open to all, embodying generous hospitality and inclusion. Some may use or create communion liturgies; others may prefer a less structured or formal approach. There will probably need to be conversations about whether and when children are free to share bread and wine. As with the practice of baptism, different churches may reach different conclusions on their practices of communion. But interpreting communion as a "peace meal" might inform these conversations and shape the practices that emerge.

The website of the Anabaptist Mennonite Network contains some liturgies and other resources for communion that embody Anabaptist emphases. One of these is a table liturgy—prayers, songs, readings, and reflections that set communion in the context of a real meal and emphasize its relational dimension. Called simply "Gathering around the Table," this resource has been used and adapted by churches and communities in many different places. A version of this liturgy appears in appendix 3. As you read it, you might reflect on how you respond, note some distinctive Anabaptist elements, and maybe think about how you could use or adapt this liturgy in your own community. Or you might be inspired to create your own "peace meal" liturgy.

HOSPITALITY
Eating together, regardless of whether the meal includes communion, is an important aspect of the hospitality and shared lives that are likely to characterize emerging Anabaptist

communities. And not just Anabaptist communities. Many emerging churches in the past twenty years have gathered around food, some of them recognizing instinctively that this builds community, others attuned to the prevalence of eating together in the Gospels. Food-based hospitality is, I believe, reshaping the church. This is eroding formal, institutional Christianity and encouraging the emergence of a relational and multivoiced community, where real friendship, rather than insipid "fellowship" or formal "membership," binds people together, sustains faith, nurtures discipleship, and builds resilience. In the challenging environment of post-Christendom, nothing less will suffice.

An emphasis on hospitality and shared meals may not, then, be distinctive of new Anabaptist communities, but it is certainly typical. *The Naked Anabaptist* identified as one of the valued aspects of the Mennonite contribution to neo-Anabaptists "the tradition of hospitality that recognizes the crucial place of eating together in building and sustaining community."[11] To what extent did the early Anabaptists value and practice hospitality? We don't have as much information as we would like about their community practices. However, as they generally met in homes and aspired to be supportive, multivoiced, and mutually accountable communities, it is inconceivable that food and hospitality were not integral, as they were in the early churches. And, like the early Christians, they were accused of holding meetings characterized by revelry and debauchery.

Regardless of whether this tradition can be traced back to the early Anabaptists, Mennonite practices and writings on the subject were very influential in attracting British and Irish Christians to Anabaptism. A surprising number of those whom Alan Kreider and I invited to tell their stories for our book, *Coming Home*, cited Mennonite cookbooks, rather than theological tomes, as points of connection. The generous hospitality offered by the London Mennonite Centre over several decades was where many of us discovered the Anabaptist vision.

When I have been invited by North American Mennonites to explain the surprising emergence of an Anabaptist network in the UK, I have always identified hospitality as a key component. Not surprisingly, one of the books in our After Christendom series is *Hospitality and Community after Christendom*. All the Anabaptist study groups that have met in homes over the past thirty years have shared meals together as well as engaged in animated conversation. Some have used table liturgies. Hospitality—eating together and welcoming anyone and everyone—is a foundational practice of SoulSpace, an emerging Anabaptist church in Bristol, and the gathering of its sister community, SoulSpace in Belfast, is called The Table.

Anabaptist networks in other nations have also identified hospitality as a common practice. Matt Stone from the Anabaptist Association of Australia and New Zealand (AAANZ) commented in relation to the tentative list of common practices we shared with our colleagues there: "I think more could be said on hospitality. Although the document mentions communion and mutual aid, I think the commitment we evidently share toward hospitality could be made more explicit." For him, this included both formal "table fellowships" and informal community-building.[12] And I was very grateful to participate in a conference hosted by the Anabaptist Network in South Africa in 2018, where hospitality was the main theme.

Both networks have engaged in sustained theological reflection on the practice and significance of hospitality, not least on the meaning of the term *philoxenia* ("love of the stranger") and its poignancy in contexts of xenophobia, racism, and hostility toward outsiders. Stone wrote: "It's encouraging to be part of a network where refugees are welcomed, where visitors from out of town are made to feel at home, where you are treated as family." Members of the AAANZ have been actively involved in initiatives to welcome refugees and to protest against alienating policies. Two of the chapters in Doug Hynd's *Community Engagement after Christendom* are focused on the Love Makes a Way movement that advocates for changed policies toward refugees and asylum seekers and practices hospitality.[13] And Juliet Kilpin's chapter in this book tells the story of a British initiative to welcome refugees that was inspired by her Anabaptist convictions.

We might also want to reflect further on the gospel stories of Jesus at table, noting that he was sometimes the host but more often the guest. In the Christendom era, the church assumed the powerful role of host. In our post-Christendom context, in which Christian communities are now minorities on the margins of society, we may more often be the guest. The Latin term *hospes* means both "host" and "guest." Letty Russell, in her book *Just Hospitality*, concludes that "hospitality is a two-way street of mutual ministry where we often exchange roles and learn the most from those whom we consider different or other." Noting that the Indo-European root of this word, *ghosti*, means host, guest, and stranger, Russell writes that "hospitality can be understood as solidarity with strangers, a mutual relationship of care and trust in which we share in the struggle for empowerment, dignity and fulness of life."[14]

Maybe, then, hospitality should be named as a further common practice alongside those we have identified. Or perhaps it should be understood as an expression of two of our common practices—an extension of our understanding of communion as a peace meal to other shared meals, and an aspect of the practice of mutual aid, discussed further in chapter 5. Either way, hospitality is not just about meals with our friends or shared church lunches but is a missional practice, a commitment to those who are on the margins and liable to be overlooked or rejected, and a mode of peacemaking. And if it is to be truly missional, it will also be culturally appropriate. In many places, this will mean offering or receiving an invitation to dinner in the host's home, but in others it may not. In some neighborhoods, only close family members enter each other's homes, and in others, meals around a dining table are unfamiliar. Some guests (or hosts) might also struggle with eating disorders or have allergies, intolerances, or foods they will not eat for religious, ethical, or health reasons. Missional hospitality will require sensitivity and creativity.

If our practice of hospitality is to be missional, and if communion is to be celebrated in the context of real meals, there may well be occasions when not all those around the table are followers of Jesus. In more formal settings, many churches indicate that only those who are committed Christians should participate and ask others to refrain from taking bread and drinking wine. Some regard this as their responsibility so as not to expose others to the risk of participating "in an unworthy manner" and thus eating and drinking judgment against themselves (1 Corinthians 11:27–29). But this is an unhelpful application of Paul's teaching. As noted, Paul was concerned about injustice and division within the community at Corinth. There were evidently "outsiders" in the meetings at Corinth (1 Corinthians 14:16), and Paul was concerned about how the church welcomed them, but he said nothing about restricting them from sharing bread and wine.

Communities that celebrate communion in the context of meals with invited guests will want to consider what to say to these guests. At the very least, this is an opportunity to explain the significance of the bread and wine for followers of Jesus. Some communities might then simply leave their guests to decide whether to participate. Others might encourage them to take bread and wine as an indication that they are on the journey, even if they have not yet decided to follow Jesus. John Wesley, founder of the Methodist movement, described communion as a "converting ordinance" and encouraged his followers to welcome all to the table.[15] It might be that emerging Anabaptist communities will practice communion in various ways, sometimes open to all, at other times for covenanted members only, when we recall and recommit ourselves to the baptismal pledges of discipleship, mutual accountability, and participation.

3

MULTIVOICED CHURCH

Three of the common practices identified by the Anabaptist Mennonite Network focus on how Anabaptist communities listen to each other, exercise discernment, reach decisions, and understand leadership. These are multivoiced worship and biblical interpretation, nonhierarchical leadership, and consensual decision-making. None of these practices were operative within the mainstream churches in the Christendom era—indeed, such widespread enfranchisement of congregations would have been regarded as dangerous and destabilizing. Dissident movements that adopted these practices on the basis of their coherence with the teaching of the New Testament were suppressed for various reasons, but their multivoiced approach was undoubtedly threatening to those who sought to control opinions and maintain centralized authority.

Examples from earlier dissident movements indicate that these practices were not Anabaptist innovations but familiar features of an older and broader radical tradition. The Waldensians, who emerged in the late twelfth century in France and spread to other parts of Europe, encouraged all their members, men and women, to preach and teach, celebrate communion, exercise leadership within their churches, and bear witness to others. They recognized certain members as leaders but did not require ordination, resisted hierarchical structures, and called their leaders *barbes* ("uncles") to differentiate them from the "fathers" of the Catholic churches. The Lollards, who flourished in England during the second half of the fourteenth century, also rejected the hierarchical structures of the state churches, chose leaders on the basis of their gifts and characters, and expected all their members, women and men, to participate actively in biblical interpretation and other aspects of their communities.

Anabaptists who adopted these practices, unaware that they were part of this radical tradition, also did so on the basis of their interpretation of the New Testament and their conviction that the Holy Spirit would empower and guide their communities. This has been true of many more recent movements. What has also been common in the development of such communities, including the Anabaptists, is the gradual drift or deliberate transition toward hierarchical structures, clericalism, diminished emphasis on the work of the Spirit, and restrictions on who can do what. The three common practices we are considering in this chapter have resurfaced persistently throughout the centuries but usually revert to default structures and expectations as the movements that pioneer them lose their initial fervor and radicalism. But in post-Christendom contexts, neo-Anabaptists have cultural, as well as biblical and missional, reasons for adopting these practices and guarding against their erosion.

MULTIVOICED WORSHIP AND BIBLICAL INTERPRETATION

Entry into an early Anabaptist community at baptism, as we noted in the previous chapter, implied readiness to participate actively in all aspects of the community. This is very different from inherited forms of church in which "going to church" was for many the only form of ecclesial activity and generally meant little beyond mere attendance or perhaps joining in with prescribed singing and liturgical prayers and actions. This is not to imply that such formal participation was necessarily insincere or meaningless, although reports of misbehavior and of sleeping through services suggest that not all were fully attentive or engaged. In our post-Christendom context, in which "going to church" is entirely voluntary, formal participation of this kind in churches that still operate in clerical Christendom mode is presumably meaningful and edifying for those who choose to attend. But this is very different from the multivoiced informal participation expected and experienced in the Waldensian, Lollard, or Anabaptist communities.

Many newer churches, especially those influenced by charismatic renewal over the past sixty years, have initially enfranchised their members and encouraged multivoiced participation. However, this has usually diminished over time, especially in churches that experience significant numerical growth, as their leaders attempt to exercise greater "quality control" and the gatherings become more predictable. The ethos and liturgical form may seem very different from the older churches, but mono-voiced preaching and front-led singing and praying may disempower communities just as effectively and result in passivity, spectatorism, or active participation only in prescribed ways. The default approach established over many centuries is difficult to resist for long. As I indicated in an earlier chapter, most of the Mennonite churches with which I have worshiped in Europe and North America retain only vestiges of the participatory ethos I associate with most early Anabaptist gatherings.

Emerging Anabaptist communities that embrace multi-voiced worship and biblical interpretation will undoubtedly experience pressure to conform, so we will need to draw on our heritage as a resource for continuing nonconformity and understand why this alternative practice is biblically rooted, culturally appropriate, missionally potent, and effective in nurturing discipleship.

My wife, Sian, and I wrote a book together several years ago entitled *Multi-Voiced Church*, which offered a rationale for this practice, gave examples from churches we knew, and explored its possibilities and pitfalls. We reflected on some of the implications of the outpouring of the Holy Spirit on the day of Pentecost and of the instructions Paul gave to the church in Corinth as he penned the most extensive account of early church gatherings in the New Testament. We recalled the popularity of this chapter (1 Corinthians 14) among the early Anabaptists and reported on their practice of multivoiced worship and the encouragements their leaders gave to this. We offered this definition of multivoiced worship:

> Multi-voiced worship anticipates that God may speak or act through any member of the church for the benefit of the whole community. It recognizes that no one person or small group has a monopoly on this. It welcomes the richness and diversity that flows from multiple contributions. It values the different perspectives, insights, angles of vision, experiences and convictions that different members bring. It does not require that all contribute or that all participate equally; nor is leadership abolished. But the ethos of multi-voiced worship is very different from corporate worship that consists of one or very few voices or allows wider participation only through pre-ordained words or actions.[1]

The term *worship* can, of course, be used in broader and narrower ways—it may describe activities that take place when followers of Jesus gather together and offer praise and prayer to God, or it may denote the conviction that the whole of our lives are to be expressions of adoration and availability to God. Although the narrower meaning is primarily in view here, one reason for encouraging multivoiced participation when the community is together is the likelihood that this will spill over into other spheres of life.

We did not offer a definition of multivoiced biblical interpretation in our book, but replacing *worship* with *biblical interpretation* in the above definition provides this. Reflecting together on the Bible and exploring its application to our communities and our lives is an expression of worship. Rather than listening passively to sermons and pondering individually how to apply what we have heard, multivoiced interpretation involves conversation, learning together, sharing insights, and testing applications. It does not preclude preaching and teaching, any more than multivoiced worship has no place for gifted musicians or liturgists. But it makes room for many perspectives and for some measure of accountability as the community focuses on applying as well as understanding the texts.

Neo-Anabaptist communities in post-Christendom contexts need not restrict multivoiced biblical interpretation to our own or similar contexts. Postcolonial studies have demonstrated the extent to which our culture influences the questions we bring to the Bible and how we understand it. Engaging with interpreters and communities in other cultures, especially those experiencing poverty, oppression, and the legacies of colonialism, may help us challenge familiar interpretations and be open to fresh, challenging, and liberating perspectives. An intriguing example of this is the collection of essays and reflections in *Unsettling the Word*, edited by Canadian Anabaptist Steve Heinrichs.[2] And postcolonial commentaries are now available on every book of the Bible.

The foundation for multivoiced church is a conviction that the Holy Spirit is at work throughout the community, that inspiration is not restricted to a few leaders (or just one), that we need the contributions of all to develop a healthy community, and that participation is much more likely to result in nurturing mature disciples. This implies that multivoiced church is appropriate in any and all contexts, but we believe there are additional cultural reasons for these practices in post-Christendom societies.

Among these are changes in educational philosophy that involve pupils in discovery and participative learning, rather than simply assimilating information; reluctance to accept the assertions of authoritative monologues; and the dialogical approach that characterizes social media and mainstream programs. We are not unaware of the challenges involved, the potential struggles and pitfalls.[3] But we believe multivoiced worship and biblical interpretation is coherent with the Anabaptist vision, and with the practice of the early Christians, and that it offers much to emerging Anabaptist communities today. Furthermore, we believe that it also has missional significance: those who have participated in biblical interpretation and other aspects of worship within the Christian community are more likely to speak about their faith with family, friends, and neighbors.

SHARED LEADERSHIP
Multivoiced church does not require the gift of leadership to be marginalized, but it does mean the roles of those with leadership responsibilities need some rethinking. Cultural changes

in Western societies are already prompting many discussions about leadership structures, processes, values, and expectations in the churches. Some are drawing heavily on secular studies, business practices, and the writings of those regarded as leadership gurus in an emerging culture, looking for models that can be imported into church circles. Popular concepts include servant leadership and transformational leadership. These terms were coined in the 1970s by Robert Greenleaf, a management consultant, and James Downton, a sociologist.[4] There is much to be learned from these sources, but many are wary of uncritically translating these secular approaches to leadership into church settings. Some argue for a more visionary, decisive, and authoritative leadership in churches; others advocate what is sometimes called "post-heroic" leadership, which is more agile, collaborative, and supposedly more in tune with contemporary culture.[5] And in a plural society, different forms of leadership may resonate more or less strongly with different cultures or age groups.

Communities inspired by the Anabaptist vision will be influenced not only by the implications for leadership of operating in a multivoiced way, but by our practice of "starting with Jesus" in our interpretation of biblical perspectives on leadership. In the biblical narrative that stretches over many centuries, there are diverse examples of leadership, good and bad, and plenty of instruction and advice given to leaders. In the New Testament, various terms are used to denote leaders, encouragements and warnings are given, and diverse interactions occur between recognized leaders and their communities. Churches through the centuries have selected approaches to leadership that have been most congenial in their contexts. In the Christendom era, notions of kingly and priestly authority undergirded the partnership between church and state. But in post-Christendom, this understanding of authority feels as outdated as that era's legacies of patriarchy and colonialism.

Anabaptist communities will want to listen to what Jesus said about leadership and reflect on the leadership he modeled. We will take note of his warning that leadership among his followers should be exercised very differently from "the kings of the Gentiles," who lord it over others and present this as being for the benefit of those they dominate (Luke 22:25–26). In this poignant exchange just before Jesus is arrested, he advocates an upside-down perspective in which leaders are servants, just as he was. John's account of the same evening recalls Jesus washing the feet of his reluctant disciples, taking the place of a servant, and urging his disciples to follow his example (John 13:1–17). Many Anabaptist communities through the centuries have taken this quite literally, washing one another's feet as an expression of mutual service and humility. Neo-Anabaptist communities today may also choose to do this or to explore culturally appropriate alternatives.[6]

The term *servant leadership*, although initially adopted from business circles, has been regarded as congruent with biblical values and is popular in Christian teaching on leadership, drawing on these gospel references.[7] While this is a genuine attempt to capture the essence of Jesus' example and teaching, the term has perhaps been overused and may carry some less than helpful connotations. These might include downplaying one's gifts, abdicating responsibility, seeking approval, displaying false humility, or even manipulating the community. Some also express concern that the characteristics usually associated with servant leadership—listening, consulting, empowering, supporting, building community, and seeking consensus—may more easily be associated with the instinctive approach of many female leaders and that this risks stereotyping them and discouraging creative, courageous, and inspiring female leaders.

Transformational leadership is also offered as an interpretation of the leadership modeled by Jesus.[8] This is often contrasted with *transactional leadership*, where the focus is on functionality and achievement. Transformational leadership, however, pays more attention to the growth and development of those who are being led and their ability to see the big picture and commit themselves to this vision. Jesus, it is suggested, was not only interested in what his disciples could achieve under his direction. He was also concerned to see them thrive, grasp his vision of the kingdom of God, and become mature. The concept of transformational leadership has also provoked criticism, not least because of its unidirectional thrust and the likelihood that leaders may attempt, wittingly or not, to "transform" their followers into their own image. Leaders also need to be open to transformation through their interaction with others, especially if they belong to communities committed to mutual accountability.

Significant as these criticisms are, the explicit link in the Gospels and elsewhere in the New Testament between leading and serving will shape emerging Anabaptist communities, as this has shaped others. These communities will also encourage leadership gifts that empower others and draw out the contributions of the whole community, rather than dominating proceedings. Those who have leadership skills can act as catalysts and facilitators. The communities can recognize that informal and formal leadership may be exercised by many members of the community, deferring to one another and seeking synergy, rather than defending their territory. This does not mean pretending that communities are leaderless: unacknowledged leadership is often manipulative and highly dangerous. But

Anabaptist communities can honor and value those with leadership gifts and experience without conforming to inherited hierarchical patterns or disempowering other members of the community.

Listening to Jesus, Anabaptist communities might also reflect on a passage that has been mostly ignored by churches of all denominations: "But you are not to be called rabbi, for you have one teacher, and you are all students. And call no one your father on earth, for you have one Father—the one in heaven. Nor are you to be called instructors, for you have one instructor, the Messiah" (Matthew 23:8–10). Titles and terminology are powerful. Ordination sets apart so-called clergy and laity. Attempts may be made to affirm "the ministry of all" or to minimize the gap, but the challenge of Jesus' teaching remains. Anabaptist communities might adopt various strategies: equating ordination with baptism; laying hands on members whenever they take on new responsibilities in church or society; rejecting the language of clergy and laity;[9] and using functional language for leadership roles. As one example, Urban Expression, a missional community shaped by Anabaptist values, refers to the members of its core team simply as "coordinators," has chosen to have no full-time leaders in its twenty-six-year history, rotates the chairing of team meetings, and operates a flat pay structure.[10]

Of course, early Anabaptists ordained their leaders, and most denominations with historical Anabaptist roots continue to do so. There were differences in the early years from ordination in Catholic or Protestant circles. Leaders were chosen from the local congregation; faithful discipleship was valued above educational qualifications; and character was more important than charisma. But Anabaptists retained ordination, whether out of conviction or unreflectively following the pattern of previous centuries. Dissenting movements cannot address every issue in the first generation! But maybe neo-Anabaptists in post-Christendom contexts can challenge the continuing practice of clerical ordination and terminology in older Anabaptist communities. Some might also search for other terms that avoid clerical connotations but are less functional and anodyne than *coordinators* and resonate with Jesus' teaching on leadership.[11]

CONSENSUAL DECISION-MAKING

The third component of multivoiced church that might characterize neo-Anabaptist communities flows naturally from the first two. Communities need to make decisions on all kinds of issues and need also to establish practices that enable good decision-making. A commitment to consensual decision-making means that the multivoiced approach to worship and biblical interpretation will also apply to making decisions. The contributions of many members of the community will feature in conversations about choices, strategies, and priorities. Skilled leadership will be required if this is to be an effective process—drawing out contributions, helping the community weigh different perspectives, discerning when and how to move from debate to decision, and making sure minority views are respected.

Two significant criticisms of an approach that aims for consensus are that this takes an inordinate amount of time and that it tends to result in conventional and conservative decisions. If the views of all members are invited and any differing views need to be carefully assessed, rather than the majority view simply being adopted or decisions being made by authorized leaders, this approach can slow down decisions and result in missed opportunities and frustration. Insistence on due process can be exhausting and may cloud the issue under discussion. An American friend commented, on the basis of his experience in several congregations, that "process is the Mennonite drug of choice." And if a community chooses to wait until everyone is agreed, this will not only delay decisions but also risk the community moving forward only at the pace of its more conservative or cautious members.

These are serious concerns, which some communities inspired by the Anabaptist vision have experienced and struggled with. Others have examined consensual decision-making and concluded that it is unwieldy and idealistic. Although in principle it enfranchises the whole community and anticipates the Holy Spirit speaking through many members and leading the community into united decisions, in practice there are many pitfalls. So is this worth pursuing? Is this a luxury that post-Christendom churches can ill afford if it means they become preoccupied with internal processes and are distracted from missional priorities? Does it actually quench the Spirit and result in stagnation?

Before rejecting this approach, we should acknowledge that there are drawbacks in other forms of decision-making in Christian communities. Those that entrust decisions to a leader or small leadership team may benefit from their wisdom and experience and from the relative speed with which decisions can be made. However, such decisions often fail to gain ownership in the community and in some cases have resulted in the community being led into dangerous activities. At the very least, those entrusted to make decisions on behalf of a community need to be subject to some accountability structure. Other communities operate on a supposedly democratic model, where all members are invited to participate in debates, and decisions are then made on the basis of a majority vote. *Vox populi*, it is hoped, equates to *vox Dei*. At its best, this approach enfranchises everyone, makes room for the Spirit to prompt contributions, and can reach decisions more quickly than a consensual process. But in practice this process can descend into political maneuvering, domination by vocal members, manipulation by leaders, and suppression of minority opinions. It can also result in more conservative views carrying the day. Other approaches involve consultation between local communities and the networks or denominations to which they belong. These helpfully draw on experience in other contexts and invite wider perspectives, but they can be cumbersome and bureaucratic or involve imposition from external bodies that may disempower the local community.

In reality, there is no perfect system in flawed human communities. Checks and balances are always needed, together with appropriate humility. However much we may want and claim to be guided by the Spirit, many other factors influence our decisions. So, if an Anabaptist community chooses to embrace consensual decision-making, what processes or practices might be helpful?

- Establishing guidelines at the outset—ensuring new members are familiar with these, identifying temptations and dangers, acknowledging fallibility, checking that everyone understands the process.
- Equipping the community to participate—providing training, practicing, inviting feedback, refining the process together.
- Recognizing that not all decisions need to be taken in this way—placing trust in designated members of the community to make many decisions so that the community can concentrate on the more significant issues.

- Developing practices that enable members of the community to express their views, listen well, show that they have understood and respect others' views, raise objections, reflect carefully, indicate changing opinions, and assent to decisions, whether or not they are fully persuaded. Consensus does not imply unanimity. One community organizer suggests offering four responses—love it, like it, live with it, and loathe it—and agreeing to move forward together as long as nobody loathes the decision.[12]

- Ensuring that minority views are properly represented and considered—that those who express these are affirmed and respected—and remembering that minority voices may often be prophetic. Consensual decision-making does not subscribe to *vox populi, vox Dei* (the voice of the people is the voice of God). On occasions, the minority view might be recognized as the way forward as the community reflects prayerfully on what has been discussed.

- Appointing someone to facilitate the process—not to dominate the discussion but to help the community engage well, ensure that members are neither silenced nor unduly vocal, and keep the process moving so that decisions are reached within a reasonable time frame.[13]

- Reminding the community that the goal of consensual decision-making is not simply to reach agreement but to discern the guidance of the Holy Spirit, and that this means listening to the Spirit as well as to each other.

Many of the these practices are equally relevant to other approaches to decision-making. My experience of democratic approaches is that participants would be much better equipped to participate with some training on how to do so and some agreed processes and practices. But despite the concerns expressed here, neo-Anabaptist communities may choose to learn how to do consensual decision-making well.

MULTIVOICED CHURCH: ANABAPTIST, BIBLICAL, CULTURAL?

Some readers of this chapter may suspect that the three practices we have explored owe at least as much to contemporary Western cultural sensibilities as to any biblical warrant or Anabaptist heritage. Western societies are generally averse to hierarchy, unchallengeable monologues, and authoritarian leadership. Postcolonial and postmodern perspectives question whether democratic systems are functioning properly and urge us to listen carefully to voices that are too often marginalized or silenced. The practices we have been advocating seem to fit well into this cultural context. But this does not necessarily mean that they are adopted only for cultural convenience. Perhaps postcolonial, postmodern, and post-Christendom perspectives can help us identify how traditional church practices were unduly influenced by cultural conformity in earlier eras. Periods of significant cultural transition open up space for fresh thinking. This was so in the early sixteenth century, when economic, political, social, and cultural turmoil provoked the Anabaptists, and many others, to question traditional practices and explore alternatives.

But did the early Anabaptists really pioneer the practices we have investigated in this chapter? There is only limited evidence of what happened in their gatherings, but it certainly seems that these were multivoiced and participative, and those who gave written guidance about the conduct of these meetings frequently emphasized that all were expected to take part. Furthermore, those who were recognized as teachers and leaders within the movement often included in their writings an encouragement to their readers to assess what they had written and offer corrections and further insights.[14] Nothing like this appears in the writings of their Catholic or Protestant contemporaries. Anabaptists invited and expected each other to contribute on the basis that the Holy Spirit was active in their lives and communities and would prompt one and another to share what the Spirit gave them.

As for shared leadership, as indicated earlier, the egalitarian approach in at least some of the Anabaptist communities gradually morphed into much more traditional structures. Indeed, quite early on in some branches of this diverse movement, authoritarian leaders provided direction and exercised control, sometimes (as in the Münster debacle[15]) with dreadful consequences. The Anabaptist tradition is a source of warnings as well as encouragements. Emerging Anabaptist communities in post-Christendom contexts might draw inspiration from the egalitarian instincts of the early Anabaptists, take note of the ease with which these could be abandoned, and seize the opportunity of a more conducive cultural context to embed this practice in our churches.

What about consensual decision-making? We know even less about the decision-making practices of the early Anabaptists than we do about their corporate worship, so we are mostly extrapolating from their multivoiced approach in other areas. But it seems inherently unlikely that members of the communities would not participate in discernment and decision-making if they participated in biblical interpretation—not least because their wrestling with the meaning and application of the Bible was the primary source of such decision-making. We know, too, that foundational documents were the result of dialogue and reaching agreement after debate. The Schleitheim Confession (1527), for example, several times reports that "we have been united" in respect of the topics under consideration. This translocal gathering drew together representatives from emerging congregations where different views were held and resulted in an agreed statement that would guide the congregations.[16]

But the early years (and later generations) were marked by division within and between congregations. Maintaining relationships with those who disagreed on issues—some important, some seemingly trivial—has not proved easy. Whatever principles are agreed and whatever practices are adopted, flawed human communities, as noted earlier, can subvert any system. Acknowledging this, it might be helpful for communities to talk together, preferably before disagreements arise, about how they will strive to maintain relationships and move forward together, despite serious differences of opinion and conviction. In his book addressing this subject, Christopher Landau, the director of ReSource, a ministry in the UK, suggests that churches might embrace "a theology of disagreement" and offers theological, biblical, and practical resources to help develop such a theology—for the sake of our communities and their witness in a fragmented and often polarized society.[17] He takes as foundational the "double love command" in Jesus' teaching (Matthew 22:37–39), Jesus' statement that "by this everyone will know that you are my disciples, if you have love for one another" (John 13:35), and the plea for unity in his prayer so that others would know that the Father had sent him (John 17:23). Urging members of the church to cultivate gracious modes of speaking, to pursue peace, and to practice "loving disagreement," Landau concludes that "an integral part of its mission . . . is to disagree Christianly."[18]

Urban Expression coordinators and mission partners have embraced a commitment to this. In our statement on theology and ethics, we say:

> We recognize that there will be some diversity among us—and we welcome this. Our commitment is to respect each other's views, embrace the discomfort these may sometimes create, and be open to fresh insights. . . . As and when theological, ethical or other issues arise within Urban Expression, we will look for guidance—about the issues themselves and about how to engage in conversation around these issues—to Scripture, to the experience of Christians elsewhere and to our own values and commitments. We will consult with each other and seek consensus (not necessarily unanimity but agreement to continue to work together on the basis of mutual respect, even if we do not fully agree with the decision reached).[19]

J. Nelson Kraybill, who was the director of the London Mennonite Centre during the 1990s and was involved in the early years of the Anabaptist Network, has drawn on his local pastoral experience and global encounters as the president of Mennonite World Conference to offer biblical and practical guidelines for communities that struggle to agree with each other. In his book *Stuck Together*, he recognizes that conflict within faith communities is inevitable, but he suggests this can be creative if we choose to listen respectfully to each other, embrace diversity, and commit to sticking together. This might mean our communities have something hopeful to offer in a polarized culture and a warring world.[20]

Similarly, J. Richard Jackson, minister of First Baptist Church, Moncton, in New Brunswick, reflecting on Jesus' surprising table companions and pleading for what he calls "the church of the bigger table," suggests that this means recognizing that God may be at work in different ways in people's lives, being secure enough to dialogue without rancor with those whom we disagree, acknowledging that dissent is healthy in church life, and expecting our own theology to grow and change over time.[21] As heirs of a dissenting tradition, Anabaptist communities today will surely not want to exclude or marginalize those who offer dissenting, and possibly prophetic, perspectives.

If contemporary culture in Western societies offers support for the three practices we have presented in this chapter, and Anabaptist history offers both encouragement and sobering warnings, how firm is the biblical foundation for these practices? As much as we want to learn from the Anabaptist tradition, if neo-Anabaptist communities are to emulate the early Anabaptists, we will primarily draw inspiration and guidance from the Bible—and especially the life and teaching of Jesus. We have suggested that multivoiced worship and biblical interpretation is consistent with Paul's teaching in 1 Corinthians, but we might also suggest that the dialogical way that Jesus usually taught, and the ways that he enfranchised his disciples, offer additional, and even more foundational, biblical support. We have said enough already about his teaching on leadership and the challenge this presents to traditional structures and practices. As for consensual decision-making, although the early churches were as prone to division as later generations, the Acts 6 and 15 accounts of how conflicts were addressed and decisions were reached offer encouraging examples.

Are these biblical, Anabaptist, and cultural arguments enough to persuade Anabaptist communities to adopt these multivoiced practices? Maybe each community will need to engage in multivoiced conversations about them. . . .

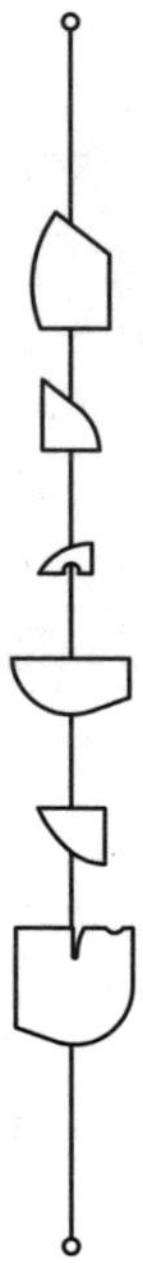

4

TRUTH-TELLING

As we continue to examine the common practices, the connections between them will hopefully become increasingly evident. We can look at them separately for the sake of analysis and clarity, but in actuality they all intersect with each other and offer, we think, an integrated approach to discipleship, community, and witness.

This chapter explores two common practices with implications for the internal health of Anabaptist communities and their witness in the world: practicing mutual accountability and telling the truth. The first of these is another expression of multivoiced church. Baptism into an Anabaptist church in the sixteenth century, as we saw in chapter 2, involved a commitment to give and receive "fraternal admonition." Mutual accountability is a more culturally appropriate way of describing this practice today—a controversial practice because it is frequently misused and is often ignored until a crisis arises. In chapter 1, we also explained why most early Anabaptists refused to swear oaths: not only on the basis of what seemed to them crystal-clear teaching from Jesus, but because they wanted to be known as those who would tell the truth without recourse to oaths.

These practices have in common the challenge of speaking truthfully for the sake of the church community and wider society. Truth-telling is a persistent concern of the biblical prophetic tradition, which calls for truthfulness in the courts and in daily life. Zechariah 8:16–17 is a trenchant example: "These are the things that you shall do: Speak the truth to one another, render in your gates judgments that are true and make for peace, do not devise evil in your hearts against one another, and love no false oath; for all these are things that I hate, says the LORD."[1] *The Naked Anabaptist* examined the practice of mutual accountability, so we need not explore it at great length here, but it said much less than it might have about the commitment to truth-telling that was as troubling to the authorities in the sixteenth century as the early Anabaptists' approach to economics and nonviolence. Telling the truth and mutual admonition, despite struggles and uncertainties, have continued to be vital practices within the Anabaptist tradition.

TELLING THE TRUTH

Those who testify in English law courts are invited to declare: "I swear by Almighty God that the evidence I shall give shall be the truth, the whole truth and nothing but the truth." Similar commitments are made in other jurisdictions. Traditionally, this oath is taken while holding or placing one's hands on a Bible. As the Christendom era fades, it is not surprising that many regard this practice as anachronistic. For most witnesses, this implies calling on a God in whom they do not really believe and promising to tell the truth in order to avoid divine judgment they do not anticipate or fear. Ironically, they swear on the Bible in which swearing oaths is prohibited on the highest authority.

Consequently, in a plural and increasingly secular society, witnesses are now able instead to swear on the Hebrew Bible or the Qur'an or to avoid religious terminology and simply "affirm" that they will speak truthfully. Affirmation, as an alternative to swearing an oath, is available in many contexts today, but oaths remain the norm in a remarkable number of situations. These include oaths sworn by people becoming doctors, veterinarians, members of Parliament, police officers, or soldiers; oaths sworn by immigrants becoming citizens; and oaths sworn by clergy promising obedience to their superiors and (at least in the UK) loyalty to the monarch. Although oaths are no longer used in business circles, many legal processes also still employ the language of oaths. And 6 May 2023 witnessed the extraordinary spectacle of the coronation of Charles III, an extravagant ceremony conducted by the state church, replete with feudal overtones. For the first time, leaders of other faith communities were represented, signaling the religious plurality, if not the secularity, of our post-Christendom society. A much more surprising innovation was the invitation to members of the public watching at home to swear an oath of allegiance to the king.[2]

But these are mere vestiges of a sacral culture where oaths were fundamental to the ordering of society, loyal citizenship, business transactions, the judicial system, and the defense of the realm. When the Anabaptists challenged the practice on the basis of what Jesus had taught, their contemporaries were outraged, fearing that if oaths were abandoned, social and political chaos would result. The Swiss reformer Heinrich Bullinger insisted: "The oath is the button, which holds together the authorities and covenants, relationships of obedience, etc. So if you now take away the oath, this is all dissolved, counts for nothing, and altogether becomes nothing, resulting in such complete confusion and disorder that it is impossible to describe."[3] Jesus had forbidden the swearing of oaths, and the early churches had followed his instructions, but the Christendom system was built on the foundation of the oath (adopting this practice from ancient Greek and Roman cultures). In a mostly nominal Christian culture, swearing oaths and the threat of divine vengeance were perceived as vital to guarantee at least some measure of truth-telling, honesty in business, and political allegiance.

How does all this relate to the practice of telling the truth today? Two expressions that have become familiar in recent years and point to the profound challenge we face in relation to truth-telling are "economical with the truth" and "post-truth." The first of these is famously associated with the UK cabinet secretary Sir Robert Armstrong, in the Australian *Spycatcher* trial in 1986. The second was named the 2016 word of the year by the Oxford Dictionaries in relation to the Brexit debate in the UK and the Trump era in America. Both expressions originated earlier but have become popular in the past thirty years, indicating widespread lack of trust in people and institutions. Add to this the conspiracy theories, distortions, irresponsible reporting, willful bias, and echo chambers of both mainstream and social media; the exaggeration and manipulation of the advertising industry; the proliferation of sophisticated criminal scams; the labeling of inconvenient information as "fake news"; the use of another expression, "I misspoke," as a euphemism for lying; institutions covering up abuse in order to protect their reputations; a former British prime minister adjudged by his peers to have repeatedly lied and misled Parliament, and so much else. It is not surprising that our culture has become cynical, suspicious, and distrustful.

Though it is deeply disappointing, it is also not surprising that church communities have been guilty of deception, manipulation, and being "economical with the truth." Some of the practices associated with traditional (and continuing) evangelistic strategies are susceptible to criticism for selectivity in what they proclaim, cultural imposition, and emotional manipulation. If we are to embrace the practice of telling the truth, we will need to begin with acknowledgment of historical failures, repentance for the damage done and the hurt caused, and proper scrutiny of our beliefs, systems, processes, and practices. While there has been some progress in recent years, especially in relation to safeguarding, much of this has resulted from external pressure and has encountered institutional resistance. Efforts to grapple with the church's legacy of involvement in oppressive colonization and profiting from the slave trade, as well as ongoing racism and abuse scandals, are still at an early stage and will require much greater truth-telling than we have yet experienced. One hopeful note was the news, while this chapter was being written, of an exhibition in the library of Lambeth Palace that lays bare the colonial legacy of the Church of England and of a £100 million fund to compensate for its historical benefit from the international slave trade. Hopefully, this will stimulate further expressions of truth-telling and repentance.

In light of these challenges, Anabaptist communities will surely want to take truth-telling seriously and recognize that we will need to proceed humbly, patiently, and persistently. In a post-truth society, learning habits of trustworthiness and engaging consistently in truthful speech will mean resisting cultural pressures. In common with other Christian communities, we will want to be honest about past failures and to be open to criticism. We will search for theological and spiritual resources to undergird our commitment to truth-telling. John D. Roth emphasizes the role of corporate worship, where we encounter afresh the truth about God and the world.[4] As we rehearse the biblical story, we also become communities of discernment and resistance, equipping each other to live faithfully and truthfully. And our communities will practice "speaking the truth in love" as a foundation for speaking truth in other contexts. Perhaps we will also choose to advocate for the abolition of oaths in post-Christendom societies, both to discourage oath-taking that often takes God's name in vain and to encourage a single standard of truthfulness in all contexts, as our sixteenth-century forebears advocated. Actually, studies of perjury (lying under oath) indicate that this has been a persistent problem through the centuries: oaths have not guaranteed truthfulness. Some emerging Anabaptist communities might champion other truth-telling causes in relation to historical abuses and contemporary practices.

But we should acknowledge that telling the truth is not always straightforward. If we look again at the wording of the oath sworn by witnesses in courtrooms, we might ask whether it is realistic or even possible for them to tell "the whole truth" in relation to whatever they witnessed. In the adversarial environment of a trial, witnesses very often are unable to tell the whole truth, because those questioning them try to restrict their answers to aspects of "the truth" that suit their purposes. Attempts by witnesses to enlarge on these answers in order to give a more adequate account are silenced. Furthermore, can any witness ever have access to or communicate the "whole truth" of even a fairly mundane incident? They may be regarded as witnesses of facts, but all "facts" involve some interpretation and perspective. "The admissible truth" has been proposed as a more realistic alternative to "the whole truth."[5]

Perhaps there are also situations where telling the truth conflicts with other ethical demands. These range from a desire not to offend someone by responding less than entirely truthfully to their enquiry about what we think of their new outfit to the much more serious dilemma of which way to direct an angry pursuer asking which way his victim went. There are biblical examples of lying to protect others that are seemingly commended. A classic example is the excuse offered by the Hebrew midwives to the Egyptian pharaoh for their failure to kill male babies. Their motivation, according to the text, was their fear of God, and the consequence was God's favor and families of their own (Exodus 1:15–21). The report of this incident is example of the subversive nature of many biblical texts: we are told the names of the midwives but not the name of the supposedly vastly more important pharaoh!

Contemplating the complexities of truth-telling, Anabaptists have reflected on a possibly apocryphal story involving Menno Simons, a Dutch leader in the early years of the movement. Traveling by stagecoach, he was riding with the driver, rather than sitting inside. The stagecoach was stopped by soldiers hunting for Menno, who was wanted by the authorities. They called out: "Is Menno Simons in the coach?" One of the passengers answered that he was not. From his seat outside Menno said, "They say Menno is not in there," and the soldiers rode off. Menno technically told the truth, but his words deceived and frustrated the soldiers. Pondering this story, Alan and Eleanor Kreider, for thirty years Mennonite mission workers in England, ask what Menno should have done. Was he being "economical with the truth"? They also note that this story has led to what in English is known as a "white lie" being called a "Mennonite lie" in the Netherlands![6]

We should also recognize that truth-telling may be understood differently in different cultures and should be wary of insensitively imposing a Western perspective on others. Both my wife and I recall conversations with people in Asian contexts where someone said they had done something when they had not but were fully intending to. From their perspective, they had spoken truthfully.

Rather than advocating a legalistic approach to telling the truth, then, Anabaptist communities may choose to reflect on this issue together—sharing experiences and perspectives, debating ethical conundrums, and supporting each other's efforts to live and speak truthfully in a post-truth culture. Our communities may also help their members discern and resist the influence of the lies, distortions, exaggerations, and manipulation of advertisers, politicians, and social influencers. They may encourage truthful speech in daily exchanges and challenge phrases such as "to be frank" or "to be honest," which imply that frankness and honesty are not required in other contexts. And, committed to "starting with Jesus," we will be eager to reflect on what Jesus said about telling the truth and what the gospel writers report in relation to his practice:

- Jesus' prohibition of swearing oaths was accompanied by the instruction to speak plainly and truthfully—so that yes means yes and no means no (Matthew 5:37). This appears to be the foundational principle, which should guide us regardless of complexities and difficult situations.
- John records Pilate's cynical question, "What is truth?" (John 18:38), which has a very postmodern feel, but in this gospel, Jesus also twice challenges his opponents on the basis that there is such a thing as truth and that he has told the truth but they have refused to accept this (8:45; 18:23).
- Matthew, Mark, and Luke all record an encounter with representatives of the religious authorities sent to trap

Jesus when these men acknowledge his integrity, truth-fulness, and impartiality (Matthew 22:16; Mark 12:14; Luke 20:21). To escape the trap, Jesus refuses to give a straight answer but asks a question that wrong-foots his opponents. Telling the truth, it seems, may not require capitulation to the categories or alternatives determined by others.

- John also begins his account with the declaration that "grace and truth came through Jesus Christ" (John 1:17) and records the well-known claim of Jesus to be "the way, and the truth, and the life" (14:6). And in this gospel, Jesus refers three times to the Holy Spirit as "the Spirit of truth" (14:17; 15:26; 16:13). Truth-telling is not just an ethical requirement but an expression of loyalty to Jesus and a practice that the Spirit empowers and guides.

Nothing in this chapter implies that telling the truth is unimportant in other Christian traditions or communities, but in my experience across many denominations, this subject is rarely discussed. In post-truth societies, where there is a wide-spread crisis of trust, communities known to be committed to truth-telling might be a sign of hope. Given the significance of truth-telling within the Anabaptist tradition, neo-Anabaptist communities in post-Christendom might well choose to high-light and explore this practice.

TRUTH AND POWER

Another phrase that has become familiar in communities that dissent from the status quo and embrace a vocation to a subversive and prophetic ministry is "speaking the truth to power." Although similar notions can be found earlier, this particular phrase seems to have first been used in 1942 by Bayard Rustin, a Black leader in the civil rights movement in America. Rustin was a Quaker who campaigned for social justice and against war. He insisted that "speaking the truth to power" was the main task of a religious community. This phrase resonated within the Quaker community and was used in a booklet about pacifism in 1955, entitled *Speak Truth to Power: A Quaker Search for an Alternative to Violence*. The phrase has been used by many others in recent years, including Old Testament scholar Walter Brueggemann in his book *Truth Speaks to Power: The Countercultural Nature of Scripture*. It implies a moral imperative to challenge untruth and injustice, and a commitment to nonviolent confrontation.

Although this phrase, or a similar one, is not found in early Anabaptist writings, as far as I am aware, it certainly describes occasions when Anabaptists challenged the leaders of church and state to change their behavior and fulfill their God-ordained responsibilities. Some did this in writings addressed to the civil authorities; others on trial confronted their accusers and urged them to heed biblical admonitions. The trial of Michael Sattler in Rottenburg in May 1527 and Melchior Rinck's *Admonition and Warning to All Who Are Part of the Magistracy* (probably composed in the same year) are classic examples of this. Needless to say, this approach did not endear them to their opponents.

Yet another phrase that may be regarded as an outworking of this approach is being "a voice for the voiceless." A student justice campaigning organization that has had links with Anabaptists in the UK named itself Speak,[7] taking its inspiration from Proverbs 31:8–9: "Speak out for those who cannot speak, for the rights of all the destitute. Speak out, judge righteously, defend the rights of the poor and needy." Similarly, one of the missional commitments of Urban Expression is "being a voice for the voiceless." Speaking truth to power will often mean championing those who are oppressed and marginalized, ensuring that those with power cannot ignore their concerns. At a local level and in daily conversations, it might involve challenging assumptions and opinions that denigrate others or endorse unjust and damaging policies and practices.

Neo-Anabaptist communities will undoubtedly be drawn to these phrases and the activities they encourage, rightly seeing these as further aspects of truth-telling. But we might also want to consider some limitations and complications. First, "speaking truth to power" has been overused in recent years and has become something of a cliché. It has been deployed not only by powerless and marginal communities but by those with a great deal of power who disagree with others (for example, by Donald Trump—not known for his truth-telling—in challenging his political opponents). The phrase can certainly be used to claim the moral high ground, so those who use it will need to be self-critical as well as provocative.

Second, focusing on denouncing the misuse of power and challenging injustices can distract us from living out alternative ways of behaving, building hopeful and loving communities, and proclaiming good news. We will want to be guided by the example of Jesus, who spoke truth to power on many occasions but whose primary vocation was to proclaim the good news of God's kingdom. And we will want to nurture within our communities what Brueggemann calls "a prophetic imagination," which inspires us and others to conceive of new possibilities.[8]

Third, unlike the early Anabaptists, we do not live in the Christendom era, when it made sense to challenge political leaders to act Christianly and give attention to the teachings of the Bible. In a plural and largely secular society, this approach is neither appropriate nor likely to be effective. This is not to suggest that followers of Jesus should be silent in the face of injustice and the misuse of power. But our tone of voice must be consonant with our minority status; we will offer our perspective confidently but graciously, aware that what we say will not be accorded greater respect (and maybe rather less) than what others say; and we will hope that the "truth" we speak will be received because it rings true, not because we claim divine or biblical authority for it.

Fourth, while "being a voice for the voiceless" may be necessary in some situations, it is surely preferable to enable those whose voices have been silenced to speak up for themselves. A significant example of this approach in our context is an initiative called Poverty Truth Commissions.[9] The starting point for this initiative is "Nothing about us, without us, is for us," which requires that those without power are actively involved in justice-seeking conversations with those who hold power. This initiative is a demonstration of the need to move away from the approach that dominated the Christendom era, when those with power decided what others needed with little or no consultation, to a post-Christendom approach of listening, empowerment, and genuine partnership.

Although we have much further to go, postcolonial studies and initiatives have sensitized us to the silencing of many voices and the imposition of what those in power presented as the "truth" about history, culture, and relationships. We now realize that what Europeans described as the discovery and settlement of North America was experienced as invasion, brutalization, and dispossession by those who already lived there. Stories of evangelizing the supposedly unreached continent of Africa by European missionaries mostly fail to mention the legacy of African theologians and church leaders from the early centuries; the persistence of Coptic, Ethiopian, and other African expressions of Christianity; and the growing presence of African missionaries in Europe. Neo-Anabaptist communities in post-Christendom, aware of how the early Anabaptists were for four centuries interpreted in the light of vilification by their opponents, might be especially concerned to listen carefully to these voices and amplify what they say. We will also be eager to learn from the experience of Anabaptists in the Majority World and invite their insights on theology, culture, and mission.

PRACTICING MUTUAL ACCOUNTABILITY

As a matter of integrity, and as a first step toward promoting and practicing truth-telling in society, members of Anabaptist communities will be concerned about telling the truth in our relationships with each other. The New Testament writers encourage truthfulness in all relationships within the community. This seems to be of particular concern to the author of Ephesians, who urges, "Putting away falsehood, let all of us speak the truth to our neighbors, for we are members of one another" (Ephesians 4:25). Earlier in the same chapter, this commitment to telling the truth is qualified in relation to our motives and attitudes and set in the context of the maturing of the Christian community: "Speaking the truth in love, we must grow up in every way into him who is the head, into Christ" (4:15). Truth-telling is one way that communities move beyond superficial relationships and become mature, but this must be done lovingly. Truth-telling is risky and can easily cause offense, as Paul recognized in his relationship with the churches he served. He vigorously defended his ministry in Corinth: "We have renounced the shameful things that one hides; we refuse to practice cunning or to falsify God's word; but by the open statement of the truth we commend ourselves to the conscience of everyone in the sight of God" (2 Corinthians 4:2). But he expressed concern about the impact of truth-telling in his relationship with the churches in Galatia: "Have I now become your enemy by telling you the truth?" (Galatians 4:16).

Practicing mutual accountability is an important aspect of this kind of relational truth-telling. It is also inherently risky. Although the intention is to restore fractured relationships and help one another on the journey of discipleship, there is no guarantee that those involved will behave well or respond positively. Furthermore, the process spelled out in the classic New Testament text (Matthew 18:15–17) is very brief and raises many questions:

> If another member of the church sins against you, go and point out the fault when the two of you are alone. If the member listens to you, you have regained that one. But if you are not listened to, take one or two others along with you, so that every word may be confirmed by the evidence of two or three witnesses. If the member refuses to listen to them, tell it to the church; and if the offender refuses to listen even to the church, let such a one be to you as a Gentile and a tax collector.

What kinds of sin are envisaged here? Only serious offenses or every minor issue? What if there is disagreement over what actually constitutes sin? Is this process only relevant when someone sins "against you," or is it applicable to any behavior that damages the community (those two words are not in the earliest manuscripts)? How many attempts should be made at each stage before moving on to the next? Should any power imbalances between the members involved be considered? If there has been abuse of any kind, surely it is unwise for the person who has been abused to confront the abuser alone (or even with others)? What role, if any, do leaders of the community—who are not mentioned in this passage—have in this process? What is involved in telling the church? How are those regarded as Gentiles or tax collectors to be treated, especially in light of Jesus' dealings with such people? If the process results in repentance and reconciliation, is there a process of restoration? How is forgiveness understood and expressed? Is reparation sometimes appropriate? And how does this process relate to issues of legality and safeguarding? These are just examples of the many questions a community will want to consider if it chooses to practice mutual accountability. Other New Testament texts (e.g., Romans 15:14; 1 Corinthians 5:1–13; Galatians 2:11–14; Philippians 4:2–3; Colossians 3:16; 1 Thessalonians 5:14; 2 Thessalonians 3:6, 14–15; 1 Timothy 5:19–20; Titus 3:10; James 5:19) offer further guidance, but many questions remain.

Neo-Anabaptist communities in post-Christendom societies may nevertheless decide to take the risk and commit themselves to this practice. We will do this if we are persuaded that mutual accountability is essential to develop mature communities of countercultural disciples; if we recognize our capacity for unfaithfulness and need of each other's support; if we want to cultivate deep friendships and live peacefully with one another; and if we regard this as another example of "starting with Jesus," given that this is one of only two instances in the Gospels where the term "church" is on the lips of Jesus. But this practice cannot be imposed on a community or implemented without teaching, discussion, training, reflection, and safeguards. It needs to be owned by members of the community, and its potential for healing and harming must be understood. And it needs to be examined in relation to the implications of *not* practicing this and the damage that can do in communities.

There are resources for communities to draw on if they decide to explore this practice, not least learning from other communities who have experience in this area. Within the Anabaptist tradition there are both encouragements and warnings, as there are in other traditions which have embraced this practice. The early Anabaptists were convinced that mutual admonition was essential and that the low moral standards in the state churches were a result of this practice being ignored. But their attempts to recover this practice were often characterized by harshness and disagreements as to how to apply the New Testament teaching. Mutual accountability degenerated into mutual excommunication! But over the years, wisdom has accrued, and communities exploring this practice can learn from this experience.[10]

When I have taught on this subject, people have often responded by saying that there are similarities between this practice and guidelines in their workplaces for resolving conflicts. They are encouraged to speak privately with others about issues before escalating grievance processes to other levels in the institution. There are also similarities in the processes employed by restorative justice practitioners, who attempt to bring together victims and offenders in safe places of conversation. This is not surprising, since Mennonites have been at the forefront of advocating restorative justice and equipping practitioners.[11] So although at first glance practicing mutual accountability might seem to be problematic in societies that valorize independence, toleration, and individualism, perhaps cultural analogies are now more numerous than we might imagine.

But mutual accountability is not just about broken relationships or sinful behavior. It might mean a small group of friends meeting together regularly to talk about issues of discipleship, sharing their struggles, praying for each other, and inviting each other to hold them to account as they commit to certain practices. It might mean those with responsibility for particular aspects of the community inviting feedback on what they have said and done. I have greatly appreciated having an accountability group over many years, reflecting with me on all aspects of my ministry and asking questions about my lifestyle, priorities, and relationships. My wife and I have also invited some trusted friends to talk with us from time to time about our finances, sharing with them information about our income, savings, and expenditure, and welcoming their advice on how we should be using our resources. Communities eager to develop mutual accountability might be wise to start with these kinds of practices as a foundation for the more demanding situations that will inevitably arise in all communities that want to move beyond superficial relationships.

What both of these common practices—telling the truth and practicing mutual accountability—require are communities that are concerned about the quality of their relationships and appreciate the profound influence of what members say to each other, and how they say it, on these relationships. What is needed to sustain these practices are communities willing to invest time in learning how to employ these practices graciously and consistently. What they offer is the possibility of authentic, healthy, and trustworthy communities that might be attractive to others in a distrustful and cynical culture.

5

SIMPLICITY AND SHARING

If "starting with Jesus" means that Anabaptist communities will pay special attention to the life and teaching of Jesus, as recorded primarily in the Gospels, we will be confronted again and again by parables, conversations, and instructions that pose questions about the economic implications of discipleship. It has been calculated that one in every seven verses in the Gospels addresses this topic. Many of the so-called "hard sayings" of Jesus are about lifestyle, the dangers of wealth, our responsibilities to those who are in need, contentment, and sharing generously and sacrificially. His dramatic announcement at the start of his public ministry, the "Nazareth manifesto," echoes the passion for social and economic justice of the Old Testament prophets and precludes any attempt to restrict the good news to spiritual concerns. And some of his most scathing comments and most subversive stories were rightly perceived by those who heard him as challenges to the prevailing economic system.

The parable of the pounds (Luke 19:11–27) has traditionally been interpreted as an encouragement to use our spiritual gifts to advance the cause of the gospel in the interim between the first and second comings of Jesus. But the parable concerns the use of economic resources to increase the wealth of a harsh and hated nobleman who was absent, seeking political power for himself. Those who heard this parable would have had no difficulty naming this person (Archelaus, a Herodian puppet king, had recently rushed off to Rome). The traditional interpretation, in which those who invested their "pounds" in ways that produced good returns are to be commended, does nothing to challenge an economic system where, Jesus says, "to all those who have, more will be given; but from those who have nothing, even what they have will be taken away" (v. 26). If that is the moral of the story, this passage sits very awkwardly between the encounter with Zacchaeus that ends in radical redistribution of ill-gotten gains and the account of Jesus driving the money changers out of the temple. So perhaps Luke intends us to identify the story's hero as the servant who refused to invest in a corrupt economic system and suffered the consequences.

The story of the widow's mite (Mark 12:41–44) has traditionally been interpreted as a challenge to give wholeheartedly and sacrificially. There is no doubt that Jesus commends her faithfulness as she contributes her few coins to the temple treasury. But, once again, the narrative context is important if we are to see the wider picture. Immediately before commenting on the generosity of the widow, Jesus warns his disciples to watch out for those who "devour widows' houses" (v. 40). And immediately after the parable, though obscured by the chapter break, Jesus predicts that the temple will soon be destroyed (13:2). The woman's contribution to the temple will have been in vain and the rapacious religious and economic system that has resulted in her becoming impoverished and having only a few coins left will shortly be dismantled.

The traditional interpretations supported, or at least did nothing to undermine, the equally rapacious Christendom system. Nor do they challenge the philosophy or injustices of contemporary global capitalism. Emerging Anabaptist communities in post-Christendom will want to revisit these and other gospel passages and ask to what extent familiar interpretations of Jesus' encounters, parables, and teachings have been unduly influenced and distorted by the political and economic interests of those who offered these interpretations.[1]

ECONOMIC DISCIPLESHIP

In light of this, two of the common practices that neo-Anabaptist communities in post-Christendom will explore are living simply and practicing mutual aid. Neither practice is straightforward, so our communities will need to reflect together on what they involve and how they can be implemented in liberating and contextually appropriate ways. They are deeply connected to the other practices we have discussed so far; practicing mutual aid is yet another expression of the baptismal commitment to mutual support and accountability, and we will certainly need each other's help in a culture of individualism and consumerism if we are to find authentic ways of living simply. Once again, these common practices are not invitations to heroic individual discipleship but opportunities for communities of disciples to support each other in exploring Jesus' teaching and developing countercultural reflexes and strategies.

Two popular approaches to economic discipleship that are deeply problematic are tithing and charitable giving. Both represent attempts to share resources and restrict personal expenditure, but neither resonates with the teaching of Jesus, and neither requires living simply or mutuality. We noted in an earlier chapter that there is no support for the practice of tithing in the New Testament or in the early churches. This practice is a legacy of the enormously expensive and oppressive Christendom system, when tithing operated as a regressive form of taxation and resulted in impoverishment and misery. Tithing is now voluntary, of course, and treasurers in most churches and denominations would be delighted if more of their members actually tithed. But this system has serious defects.

- First, tithing is a minor component in an integrated Old Testament economic system. It is proportionate and liberating only in the context of the jubilee legislation that is at the heart of that system (Leviticus 25). Extracted from this context and applied on its own, it is legalistic, unjust, and oppressive.

- Second, it is extremely good news to those of us who are wealthy if we only have to give away 10 percent of our wealth, but it is very bad news to those who are struggling to survive on limited resources. It does nothing to address our inequitable economic system or disparities in our churches.

- Third, tithing generally only involves setting aside a percentage of income. It does not require us to question how we earn this income, what we do with the rest of it, what we spend or save, where we invest our money, how this might impact a fragile environment, and how we use other resources, including our time, homes, and possessions.

- Fourth, tithing can lull us into a false complacency that we have escaped the lure of Mammon (the only evil spiritual power that Jesus names) and are living justly and generously in a global economic system that is corrupt and broken.

- Fifth, tithing is an individualistic practice that requires no consultation with others but simply a mathematical calculation. It avoids conversations about lifestyle, priorities, community, and justice.

Charitable giving, like tithing, has a long history and remains popular in secularized Western societies, where people of different faiths and none respond generously to appeals to support a very wide range of projects and causes. I began drafting this chapter the day after the televised climax of the annual "Children in Need" appeal in the UK, which raises millions of pounds and involves many thousands of people in all kinds of sponsored activities. We are bombarded by appeals from many charities to support initiatives they are championing, most of them entirely worthy. And a recent report that there are now more foodbanks in the UK than McDonald's restaurants[2] is testimony to the generosity of those who contribute food and volunteer to staff these essential resources in a time of austerity, political inertia, and food poverty.

But charitable giving has a number of drawbacks, some of which were mentioned in *The Naked Anabaptist*. As with tithing, charitable giving is usually individualistic and does not involve the community; charitable giving, again like tithing, does not raise questions about lifestyle and the use of all our resources; charitable giving is one-way and usually at arm's length, rather than relational; and charitable giving does not address issues of economic injustice within society or globally. Neo-Anabaptists in wealthy post-Christendom societies are beneficiaries of a distorted and unjust global economy that is maintained by imperial systems which are just as oppressive as the Roman Empire that backdropped the life of Jesus and the New Testament.

As has often been documented, charitable giving can create dependency, represent a form of "othering," and further disempower those who receive it. Food banks are an essential resource for thousands of families in the UK, but they are also an indictment on a wealthy society that does not share its resources equitably. Structural changes are needed, which the provision of food banks might unwittingly discourage by reducing the pressure on governments to act. Similarly, at an international level, reparations are needed for the damage caused by the slave trade and, more recently, to the climate by Western nations.[3] These are matters of justice, not charity.

Tithing and charitable giving, while flawed, are much better than nothing. Both may represent generous, even sacrificial, giving. But they are inadequate responses to the teaching of Jesus and may distract us from more radical and liberating practices, and from the dynamics and potential of mutual aid. For many followers of Jesus, the problem is exacerbated by the amount given to support the church—its staff, premises, and programs. Arguably, these gifts are not actually charitable (and so tax relief should not be claimed on them), as the donors are also beneficiaries of what they have given. Do we really need to spend so much on ourselves? This is where the common practice of living simply may influence our choices.

LIVING SIMPLY

Although the expression *living simply* is not found in the New Testament, it is certainly implied in various places. A very familiar passage in the Sermon on the Mount sets out Jesus' perspective. Having already urged his disciples not to store up treasures on earth (Matthew 6:19), Jesus tells them not to worry about the necessities of life or to strive after things, instead, trusting their heavenly Father (6:25–33). The petition in the Lord's Prayer for "our daily bread" (6:11) likewise suggests that necessities, rather than luxuries, should be our priority. In many other places, it is clear from Jesus' teaching that wealth is a hindrance to faith and discipleship.

Elsewhere in the New Testament, similar teaching is found. The rarely discussed and (in our society) notably countercultural notion of "contentment" is at the heart of the spirituality commended in many passages: "I have learned to be content with whatever I have" (Philippians 4:11); "There is great gain in godliness combined with contentment" (1 Timothy 6:6); "If we have food and clothing, we will be content with these" (1 Timothy 6:8); "Keep your lives free from the love of money, and be content with what you have" (Hebrews 13:5). Living simply is an invitation to freedom from anxiety, striving, competition, envy, encumbrances, and cupidity. Contentment does not mean passivity but liberation from unnecessary concerns in order to release time and energy for loving God and our neighbors (activities that, according to Jesus, are to be our primary pursuits and how we fulfill all the commandments; Matthew 22:37–40). Freedom from serving Mammon sets us free to serve God (Matthew 6:24).

Another term not found in the New Testament is *uncluttered*, but this features in Urban Expression's statement of core values: "We realize the importance of living uncluttered lives, holding possessions lightly and recognizing that all we have is to be at God's disposal." Cluttered homes are now so prevalent in the UK that it is possible to earn a living as a professional declutterer. As we are daily encouraged by advertisers to buy more and more possessions, refusing this and choosing to simplify our lives and homes is an act of cultural resistance. But it is liberating, as those who have employed a declutterer testify. And decluttering is not limited to possessions. It might be just as liberating to declutter our diaries. I am frequently contacted by people who apologize for interrupting my busy schedule, but I do not regard myself as unduly busy. I often hear others complaining about how busy they are, but I am not very sympathetic. While I recognize that periods of busyness are inevitable for most people, and that for many people, earning enough to pay the bills involves multiple jobs or more hours at work than they would wish, for many of us busyness is a choice, sometimes a badge of honor. But this is likely to be unhealthy, counterproductive, and dehumanizing. Uncluttering our calendars may be a significant aspect of living simply.

The term *uncluttered* appears in another of the Urban Expression core values: "We are committed to uncluttered church." Do our churches need all their facilities, staff, and programs? Do we need our own buildings at all? Could we release time, energy, and resources for more creative and missional activities? Perhaps one of the important lessons from the periods of pandemic restrictions in 2020 and 2021, when church buildings were closed for months and many programs were either cancelled or moved online, is that we need not be bound by inherited patterns. There were things we could not do in those periods, but we discovered different ways of meeting and engaging with local communities. And, although many churches have already reverted to familiar practices, others are determined to seize the opportunity to reimagine themselves. Many will have no option. Recent research suggests that significant numbers of people have not returned to church after the lockdowns, that others are no longer willing to volunteer in the same way, and that there has been a serious reduction in church income. The research also indicates that, for many people, the lockdowns provoked them to question why they were doing what they were doing and convinced them they could not continue. Church programs were too cluttered, and they were close to burnout.

We will undoubtedly be processing the experience of the COVID-19 pandemic and its challenges for many years, but one early outcome may be the emergence of simpler expressions of Christian community. There have been movements in this direction for several years, with many advocates of simpler forms of church. These may seem more fragile but may be more resilient and flexible in post-Christendom contexts if they are not weighed down by the maintenance of buildings and heavy programs. This approach should be attractive to neo-Anabaptist communities in light of the witness of the early Anabaptist communities, which were characterized by domesticity, pared-back forms of worship, multivoiced participation, and informality. Perhaps, together with other churches, these communities can consider two important questions: What activities are essential to *sustain* faith, discipleship, relationships, and mission; and what activities are *sustainable* with limited personnel and resources?

There are also lessons to be learned from the Amish and their critical interrogation of new forms of technology, especially their questioning of whether a gadget builds community or hinders it. But this need not mean (for the Amish or for the rest of us) total resistance to technological developments. The pandemic showed us how much can be done online through the ubiquitous digital technology. While there are limitations, remote conversations and meetings have dramatically reduced the time, cost, and environmental impact of multiple in-person meetings. It will no doubt take some time to reach a new equilibrium in relation to online and in-person activities, but this may be an example of technological advances facilitating greater simplicity and sustainability while also building multi-voiced communities in new ways.

Lurking behind this discussion, though, is the question of what living simply actually means and how we assess this. Living simply means something vastly different in different contexts, as anyone knows who has traveled widely or just spent time locally with those who have a different level of income. Legalistic approaches are unlikely to be helpful or liberating. Exploratory conversations, marked by honesty and humility, especially if these involve conversation partners in other cultures, may be much more valuable, albeit eye-opening and challenging. The emergence and growth of Anabaptist communities in the Majority World offer opportunities for such conversations that draw both on the Anabaptist tradition and on contextual insights. One helpful resource, albeit now over forty years old, is a collection of essays and case studies edited by Ronald Sider, entitled *Living More Simply*.[4] This collection is less well known than Sider's earlier book *Rich Christians in an Age of Hunger*, which also explored lifestyle issues and global justice and was very influential in the 1980s and 1990s.[5] Although all the contributors to the later book, including some Anabaptist writers, were based in North America and did not interact with global voices, it contains a wealth of biblical reflection and practical discussion. Anabaptist communities in post-Christendom societies, more alert to postcolonial perspectives, might draw on this older resource, but we will want to engage in a more international conversation.

A commitment to living simply might also be one of our responses to the climate crisis that threatens the future of humanity and is already wreaking devastation on many parts of the world. Western lifestyles have been achieved by exploiting natural resources and communities in the Majority

World. These are unsustainable, as is the expectation of continuing economic growth promoted by Western politicians. Neo-Anabaptist communities will surely want to join others in challenging this policy, exposing its dangerous assumptions, and practicing simpler ways of living. We and others will surely also want to learn from the insights of those who have been at the forefront of engaging with the challenges presented by the climate crisis. In an article published in early 2023, Evert van de Poll, professor of religious science and missiology at the Evangelical Theological Faculty in Leuven, lists several beneficial practices advocated by Christian and other environmental groups: before buying, consistently asking what we really need; choosing collective modes of transport; reducing the number and use of electronic devices; reducing our consumption of meat; choosing local food produced without chemicals; living close to the workplace, if possible; and sharing instead of owning some possessions. He argues that the call for a simpler lifestyle issued forty years ago by Sider and others needs to be heard again today in light of the ecological imperative. The practices listed here are only samples, and van de Poll wisely suggests that the relative term *simpler living* might be more helpful so that we avoid absolutes that don't work in different contexts and can focus on becoming "less consumerist, less demanding on natural resources, less destructive for eco-systems."[6]

Are there resources in the Anabaptist tradition on which we can draw? While the early Anabaptists lived in a different era and have nothing directly to contribute in relation to the climate crisis or current economic policies, the Anabaptist tradition has been characterized by a spirituality of humility, an ethic of restraint, and resistance to excess. Contemporary Anabaptists in Western societies may have become wealthy, with many choosing to live in affluent neighborhoods, but the tradition represents an uncomfortable challenge. As a movement that flourished among the disenfranchised, the Anabaptist tradition poses questions about where we choose to live and why, and how we engage with those on the margins of our societies.

PRACTICING MUTUAL AID

Living simply, then, removes distractions and hindrances to discipleship, helps us discover more sustainable forms of Christian community, and enables us to do less damage to the planet. But it also frees our resources and imaginations to enable us to share more with others. The practice of mutual aid was commended by the early Anabaptist writers and is deeply rooted in the tradition, although different groups have understood and implemented this commitment in different ways.

For some of the Anabaptist communities in Moravia, mutual aid meant renouncing private ownership and participating in a "common purse" economy. All but a few personal items were held in common ownership, and resources were distributed to members of the community as needed. Those who joined these groups surrendered their autonomy, control, and possessions. This was not a decision to be taken lightly, so newcomers were urged to consider this very carefully. Nearly five hundred years later, Hutterite communities descended from the Moravian groups still maintain this practice. In the UK and elsewhere, Bruderhof communities, inspired by but separate from the Hutterites, also operate as common purse communities.[7] And from time to time other movements or local communities adopt this practice. None of the Urban Expression teams have so far operated in this way, but some have talked about it as a way to support each other in marginal urban neighborhoods, and there have been many examples of sharing resources and liabilities.

Although this practice may have originally been adopted out of economic necessity in Moravia, very soon it was justified on the basis of the communities' understanding of the New Testament, especially the account of the first church in Jerusalem in Acts 2 and 4. It seems from the Gospels that Jesus and his disciples comprised a small and mobile common purse community, although the details are lacking. The account in Acts is more explicit and contains phrases such as "all who believed were together and had all things in common" (2:44); "they would sell their possessions and goods and distribute the proceeds to all, as any had need" (2:45); "no one claimed private ownership of any possessions, but everything they owned was held in common" (4:32); and "there was not a needy person among them" (4:34). These compelling texts witness to a radical expression of mutual aid, represent a creative application of the principles of jubilee, and appear to offer a secure New Testament foundation to the practice of common purse community.

Most other Anabaptist communities from the early years until today have endorsed the practice of mutual aid but have not expressed this in a common purse economy. Although some form of common purse community seems to have operated in the Jerusalem church, there is no evidence that other churches adopted this practice or were urged to do so. Furthermore, the account in Acts hints that this was a more fluid situation than church members renouncing all claim to their resources. The account continues: "For from time to time those who owned land or houses sold them, brought the money from the sales and put it at the apostles' feet, and it was distributed to anyone who had need" (Acts 4:34–35 NIV). The wording implies that the sharing process was ongoing, rather than a one-off commitment, and that private ownership was not regarded as illegitimate. Indeed, in the disturbing story of Ananias and Sapphira, the couple are castigated for dishonesty, but Peter explicitly affirms that their property and money were theirs and that they were under no obligation to give it to the church (Acts 5:4). Common purse communities today are authentic and challenging expressions of mutual aid, and emerging Anabaptist communities might choose to adopt this approach, but their supposed New Testament foundation is less persuasive than some claim.

However, the New Testament, and not least the teaching of Jesus, makes it clear that mutual aid is essential to Christian community and a mark of faithful discipleship. Giving to those in need, regardless of whether they can reciprocate, is both assumed and taught in the Sermon on the Mount (Matthew 5:42; 6:2). The parable of the good Samaritan commends the care and generosity shown to a man in distress (Luke 10:30–37). Another parable castigates those who hoard their resources and fail to share them with others (Luke 12:16–21). And meeting the needs of those who are hungry, thirsty, strangers, naked, sick, and in prison is a form of ministry to Jesus himself (Matthew 25:35–36). In none of these situations is there reciprocity. Mutual aid is not always feasible in an unequal society. Indeed, Jesus warns against only showing hospitality to those who can reciprocate (Luke 14:12–14). However, Jesus also envisages mutuality wherever this is possible. He sends out his disciples with only minimal resources so that they will need to receive hospitality from others (Matthew 10:9–10; Luke 10:4–8). He makes it clear that those who have received debt relief should extend this to others (Matthew 18:23–35). And he tells his disciples that selling their possessions to give to those who are in need benefits the giver spiritually: "Where your treasure is, there your heart will be also" (Luke 12:34).

Mutual aid is at the heart of Paul's encouragement to the church at Corinth as he urges them to contribute to a collection for the impoverished Christians in Jerusalem. He explains: "I do not mean that there should be relief for others and pressure on you, but it is a question of a fair balance between your present abundance and their need, so that their abundance may be for your need" (2 Corinthians 8:13–14). The term *koinonia* appears in many places in the New Testament. This word, literally "commonness," had a broad range of meanings, but it was essentially an economic term, denoting business partnerships, joint donations, or collections. Luke uses this term to describe the priorities of the Jerusalem church: "They devoted themselves to the apostles' teaching and fellowship [koinonia], to the breaking of bread and the prayers" (Acts 2:42). Paul uses it for both the collection [koinonia] he is making from the Corinthians and their celebration of the Lord's Supper: "The cup of blessing that we bless, is it not a sharing [koinonia] in the blood of Christ? The bread that we break, is it not a sharing [koinonia] in the body of Christ?" (1 Corinthians 10:16).

Taking up a collection, or offering, may still be a familiar practice in many churches, although funds are increasingly transferred electronically rather than by placing cash in collection bags. But it is very often accorded little attention and sometimes done almost apologetically while announcements are being made or a song is being sung. Perhaps this is a practice that neo-Anabaptist communities can revitalize—by regarding it as an act of worship, encouraging members to signal the availability of their time and other resources as well as their money on the offering plate, or by encouraging those in need to take money out of the collection bag as it passes them. They might also learn from some churches with roots in the Majority World where the offering is an opportunity for dancing and joyful celebration. What they will want to avoid, of course, is anything that smacks of pressure or manipulation, anything that prioritizes the financial needs of the institution over the well-being of their members, anything that is inconsistent with the biblical emphasis on joyful and voluntary contributions.

Koinonia is concerned with the sharing of resources, responsibility for the needs of others within the community, the just distribution of wealth, and practical action to relieve needs. Koinonia does not require the abolition of individual ownership, but it challenges how we use what we own.[8] This implies much more than tithing or charitable giving, as in the first church, when "no one claimed private ownership of any possessions" (Acts 4:32). What we own is available to those who need it, and what others own is available to us when we need it. The author of 1 John challenges us: "How does God's love abide in anyone who has the world's goods and sees a brother or sister in need and yet refuses help?" (1 John 3:17).

Koinonia also means our communities being alert to inequalities among members and encouraging sharing of resources. We might shy away from this, but even if we choose to embrace it, in a world of huge needs and gross injustice, where do we start? How do we decide what to share and with whom? Once again, rather than legalism, this is an invitation to open and humble conversations within and beyond our communities, and to mutual accountability, as we talk with others about what we have and what we and others need. Talking openly about personal finances is countercultural, almost taboo, in most social contexts (although much less so in poor neighborhoods). On several occasions I have demonstrated this by inviting members of a congregation to turn to the person next to them and share what they earn, how much they spend on their vacations, and how much they give away. Nobody moves, nor do I expect them to do so. After a short pause, I ask why we find this so threatening or embarrassing. Rather than discussing economic issues being taboo or awkward, perhaps our communities can find creative and joyful ways to subvert the individualism and consumerism that plagues Western culture.

A heightened commitment to mutuality, to giving and receiving, might be yet another outcome of experiences during the pandemic restrictions. Many churches, eager to find practical ways to engage with people in their neighborhoods, were surprised and a little discomfited to discover many other community groups and individuals already responding to needs and sharing expertise and resources. Churches were often playing catch-up and found themselves drawn into partnerships they had not initiated and were not leading. Perhaps this experience will encourage the shift needed in post-Christendom as a marginal and minority Christian community learns we no longer need, or have the capacity, to run everything or dominate initiatives. An understanding of mutual aid that extends beyond the Christian community might help us forge creative and mutually enriching partnerships with others.

Some churches have also drawn on the approach and practices of asset-based community development,[9] where the primary focus is on the gifts, skills, experiences, and resources of a community rather than its needs and deficiencies. Neo-Anabaptist communities are likely to find this approach congenial and might understand this as an extension of the practice of mutual aid. A commitment to following Jesus in bringing "good news to the poor" implies that our communities have something good to bring into our neighborhoods, so we do not come empty-handed, but we might follow the example of the early disciples in not bringing too much with us and being ready to receive from others, to be guests rather than assuming we must be hosts.

THE RICH YOUNG RULER

A familiar episode in the life of Jesus draws together some of the issues we have examined in this chapter. The synoptic gospels all record this incident (Matthew 19:16–30; Mark 10:17–30; Luke 18:18–30). Piecing the texts together, we discover that the man who approached Jesus was rich, young, and a ruler, although none of the passages provide all of these descriptions. The subject of numerous sermons, this encounter reads very differently in different contexts.

In affluent Western societies, readers or listeners are invited to identify with the rich young ruler and to heed the challenge of Jesus to simplify our lives, dispense with excessive possessions, and follow Jesus wholeheartedly. If any attention is paid to what happens to these possessions, the assumption is probably charitable giving. In contexts of poverty and injustice, readers and listeners more naturally identify with the other person in the story—someone who is almost always ignored in Western sermons—the poor person who is the designated recipient of the rich man's possessions. The outcome to which Jesus points is not charity but redistributive justice. This would be "good news to the poor" and also to the rich man, freed from his excessive wealth to live much more simply. These diverse readings remind us how important context is for biblical interpretation and how we need the insights of a global community.

The story continues with the shock the disciples experience and their uncertainty about whether anyone can enter God's kingdom. Jesus does not mince words: "It is easier for a camel to go through the eye of a needle than for someone who is rich to enter the kingdom of God" (Mark 10:25). Some readers may have heard this saying interpreted in relation to a gate in the city of Jerusalem, the Needle Gate. Those who approached the city via this gate, many preachers have explained, needed to dismount and unload their camel in order to pass through. The moral of the story, then, is that those who would follow Jesus must humble themselves and detach themselves from the love of their possessions. But there never was a Needle Gate in Jerusalem. This was invented in the Christendom era as a way of softening the impact of what Jesus said and differentiating between "having possessions" and "loving possessions." In that era, living simply was not required, merely a certain attitude toward wealth. In a post-Christendom and postcolonial context, for the sake of those who are poor and those who are rich, we need to disavow such evasions.

Seeking reassurance, Peter reminds Jesus that his followers have abandoned their homes and livelihoods to follow him. What Jesus promises in response is abundant resources, albeit with persecution, and not just in the age to come. In this age, his followers will have unimaginable prosperity. This is not the affluence promised by the so-called prosperity gospel, in which individuals aspire to become wealthy. Rather, this is the Christian community opening our homes to each other, sharing our resources, and practicing mutual aid. As a recipient of generous hospitality in many nations, where I have been welcomed into homes, sharing meals, sleeping in beds or hammocks, on sofas or mats on the floor, I consider myself tremendously wealthy to belong to such a global community. And my wife and I have had the privilege of providing such hospitality for visitors from all over the world and learning so much from our times with them. Such is the joy of mutual aid.

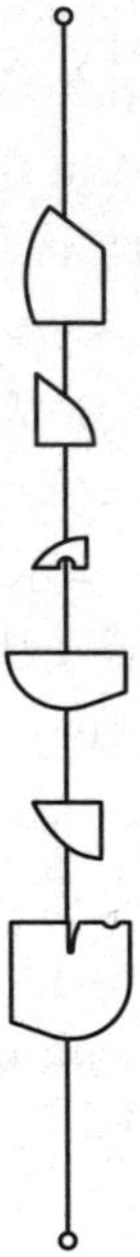

6

PEACEFUL WITNESS

This chapter explores the last two common practices that neo-Anabaptists in the UK have identified: practicing nonviolent peacemaking[1] and witness in word and lifestyle. I have had many conversations over the years with North American Mennonites about the relationship between evangelism and peace. In many contexts, the term *evangelism* is strongly disliked and distrusted,[2] at least in part because of the antics of televangelists and aggressive and insensitive practices that are all too common in North American Christianity (and certainly not absent from evangelism in the UK). Some have commented that most Mennonite churches focus on *either* peace and social justice *or* evangelism, but few integrate these. Others are concerned that emphasizing the traditional Mennonite commitment to nonviolence puts up a barrier that discourages others from joining their churches.

I have encountered similar disquiet among some European Mennonites. Several years ago, some Dutch Mennonite pastors invited me to help their aging and declining churches find ways to reach out to their neighbors—with the proviso that they did not want to adopt the practices of the local evangelical churches! In Europe and North America, Mennonites have frequently advocated the priority of witness by lifestyle, rather than verbal witness. And the witness of nonviolent peacemaking might be regarded as a significant component of this, together with efforts to respond to humanitarian needs and pursue social justice.

In several sessions with the Dutch Mennonites, I encouraged them to draw on their deepest Anabaptist roots. The earliest Anabaptists were passionate evangelists who were so vocal in their testimony that tongue screws were used to silence them.[3] We have accounts from some prominent evangelists of hundreds or thousands they had baptized. We know also of those who persistently evangelized their neighbors, even if they rarely left their homes. Neo-Anabaptists in the UK have often told the story of Margaret Hellwart, a passionate evangelist who was repeatedly chained to her kitchen floor to prevent her from sharing her faith with her neighbors.[4] But, as all members of Anabaptist communities were expected to share their faith with others, there are very many more of whom we know nothing. However, Anabaptists were also passionately committed to religious liberty and were averse to pressuring people to respond to their message. After initial uncertainty, most Anabaptists also adopted an ethic of nonviolence. Peace and evangelism can, it seems, be integrated.

Various reasons have been suggested as to why the Anabaptist tradition retained its commitment to nonviolence but lost its evangelistic passion. Severe persecution no doubt played a part, and in some places, toleration was achieved at the expense of agreements not to evangelize. Cultural assimilation later involved accepting the idea that religion is a private matter, and some Mennonites have effectively reduced their understanding of mission to various forms of social engagement. Hesitancy about verbal witness seems to have become an expression of

Mennonite identity for many, perhaps linked with an ethos of self-effacing spirituality and humility. As noted in an earlier chapter, missiology does not feature strongly in some recent summaries of Anabaptist practices, let alone evangelism.

But Anabaptism during the twentieth century became a global movement through the efforts of many cross-cultural missionaries, and many of the younger churches they planted are far less hesitant than traditional Anabaptists about sharing their faith verbally. This is true also of other Christians and churches that have been inspired by the Anabaptist vision. And there are encouraging signs among more traditional Anabaptists of fresh missional thinking and practice, including the recovery of evangelism.[5] Perhaps it is possible to be committed to both peace and evangelism. Neo-Anabaptist communities in post-Christendom contexts might find this dual emphasis helpful and attractive rather than problematic.

The term *missio Dei* points in this direction. It emerged during the mid-twentieth century and has become very influential in recent decades, at a popular level as well as among theologians and missiologists. During the Christendom era, mission was understood as an activity or program of the church, usually carried out by specialists beyond the boundaries of Europe, which was perceived as already Christian. Many who engaged in this form of mission were dedicated, passionate, and heroic, but mission in this era was marred by imperialism, colonialism, imposition, and cultural insensitivity. *Missio Dei*, in contrast, represents a post-Christendom understanding of mission. It insists that mission is a divine initiative flowing from the heart of a missional God. As followers of Jesus, we are invited to participate in this mission, but we do so aware that God is already at work beyond and before us, so we adopt a stance of listening and learning, we act and speak humbly, and we are open to receive as well as to give. *Missio Dei* also alerts us to the cosmic scope of God's mission to restore shalom to the whole of creation. Evangelism and peacemaking are not alternative strategies but integral components in this multifaceted missiology.

WITNESS IN POST-CHRISTENDOM

In a deeply skeptical culture, witness by lifestyle is essential. Most people become followers of Jesus Christ through the witness of those they know personally—friends, colleagues, or family members—who live out the gospel in winsome and persuasive ways. Authenticity is crucial. Furthermore, the witness of a community that lives out the gospel is especially attractive. Many churches have realized that people often need to "belong" for some time before they "believe." This may not seem congruent with the hard ecclesial boundaries of the Anabaptist tradition and its high expectations of what it means to be involved in and wholeheartedly committed to the community. But this "belonging" is relational and missional. It does not equate to covenanted membership, nor does it diminish the significance of baptism when people are ready to take this step of faith and discipleship. But it recognizes that in a post-Christendom context, journeys to faith may be lengthy and require neo-Anabaptist communities and other churches to be patient, welcoming, and attentive to the importance of living out the gospel.

Lifestyle witness does not, however, demand perfection from the witnesses. Indeed, the testimony of God's grace in the lives of far-from-perfect followers of Jesus might be much more attractive. Nor can we ignore the appalling shortcomings of churches, Christian institutions, and individual Christians—historical and contemporary—that are periodically highlighted by the media and present stumbling blocks. Involvement in the slave trade, oppression of minorities, sexual abuse and covering this up, financial corruption, psychological manipulation, infighting and division, and much else call for repentance, reparation, and appropriate humility in our witness. Perhaps the first priority of verbal witness is to confess and apologize that we have been such flawed witnesses to Jesus. Rick Richardson, professor of evangelism and leadership at Wheaton College, advocates for "a decolonized and decolonizing post-Christendom evangelism" and suggests that we should share our struggles, weaknesses, and failures rather than our victories.[6] This may open the way for further conversations.

Some years ago, a friend invited me to join him in a conversation with a group that had spent some weeks on an Alpha course he had hosted.[7] At the end of this introductory course on Christianity, the group had thanked him but asked if they could meet again and ask the questions they wanted to ask, rather than the ones the course assumed they had. One member of the group asked us how the gospel could be true if Christians had behaved so badly over the past two thousand years. We learned that he had asked others this question and had only encountered excuses, so he was surprised and relieved when we acknowledged the problem and explored it with the group over the next couple of hours. I have had similar conversations with others who may not know much about the gospel but are very aware of the harms perpetrated throughout church history. In post-Christendom societies, this legacy is a barrier to faith and must be acknowledged before we are likely to receive a sympathetic hearing. But consistent, albeit imperfect, lifestyle witness by both individuals and communities is a vital accompaniment to honesty about past and present failings.

As essential as witness by lifestyle is, it is not enough in post-Christendom, where people increasingly have no way of interpreting this without explanation, or in a postmodern, postsecular culture, where multiple alternative lifestyles are on offer. The Anabaptist commitment to being countercultural and distinctive is hard to apply in a decentered and diverse multiculture. Arthur McPhee, former professor of practical theology at Asbury Theological Seminary, rejects the idea that "our acts of mercy, work for justice, efforts at peacemaking, advocacy of the poor, care for creation, and other expressions of our new life in Christ are, by themselves, testimony enough." He insists that "by deeds alone we only point to ourselves."[8] Verbal witness is necessary. The 2021 UK census results were released as this chapter was being drafted, confirming what many of us assumed would be the case: for the first time since information about religious belief and affiliation was collected, less than half the population now describes themselves as even nominal Christians. Far fewer participate in our churches or have much knowledge of Christianity.[9] Most have no framework for interpreting any kind of lifestyle witness without explanation.

It is disappointing that *evangelism* is associated with so many negative images and practices, some of these obsolete legacies of Christendom and colonialism that are still remembered, others sadly still prevalent. The word itself refers to the sharing of good news, announcing something that others will welcome hearing. Whether we can rehabilitate this term or might need to use another, such as *sharing faith*, disavowing or marginalizing verbal witness will only exacerbate the decline of the churches and the advance of a culture that is "post-Christian" as well as post-Christendom. And it might just be that in the years ahead, verbal evangelism will become less problematic as we encounter more people who are entirely unfamiliar with the gospel and are interested to hear more. Over the past few years I have collected numerous anecdotes from people in several nations indicating both the depth of ignorance of Christianity of many people in post-Christendom societies and their interest in learning more about Christian faith. Curiosity, rather than hostility or indifference, has frequently been the reaction when people encounter stories, events, symbols, or buildings that are unfamiliar.

After centuries when most people knew something of the gospel, and decades when many have been uninterested in hearing more about something they vaguely knew and regarded as outdated, we may soon be in contexts analogous to those of the early Christians after they moved beyond the Jewish heartlands. Evangelism, or sharing faith, as post-Christendom advances will require us to start much further back than was necessary for the early Anabaptists, telling an unknown story and explaining alien concepts.

Neo-Anabaptist communities, then, will affirm the necessity of witness in both deed and word. Despite the noted shortcomings of the Anabaptist tradition, we might take inspiration from the passion of the early Anabaptists and may also find certain emphases in this tradition helpful in exploring ways of sharing faith. Among these is the insistence that Jesus is at the center of the Christian message; that the human life and teachings of Jesus are essential aspects of the gospel; and that it is important to answer not only the question "Why did Jesus die?" but also "Why was he killed?" This second question alerts us to the political, economic, and social reasons why Jesus was such a threat to the authorities and precludes an over-spiritualized form of evangelism. Evangelism that preaches only a privatized gospel, that fails to engage with sociopolitical and economic realities, or that differentiates too strongly between the evangelistic and prophetic aspects of mission lacks authenticity and may be a tool of oppression, unwittingly endorsing and undergirding an unjust status quo. In a post-Christendom society—where there is little interest in churches or in doctrinal statements, but the person of Jesus himself still attracts attention and admiration—it may be crucial that the evangel concentrates on Jesus, retells the full story of his life, death, and resurrection, and invites people to follow him.

The Anabaptist tradition might also encourage neo-Anabaptist communities to take care that our evangelizing is ethically responsible. The commitments to truth-telling and religious liberty that are deeply rooted in this tradition can alert us to dangers and temptations:

- Ethical evangelism means inviting without inducing. The evangelist invites people to hear the story of God's salvation and to consider the implications of this story for their own lives. These implications involve both challenges and promises. The gospel is both attractive and demanding. Ethical evangelism requires that the cost of discipleship is acknowledged alongside the benefits of faith.

- Ethical evangelism means persuading without pressuring. The evangelist tries to persuade people to respond to the invitation and challenge of the gospel. Persuasion is part of biblical evangelism; it is evident in the ministry of Jesus, the early missionaries, and sixteenth-century Anabaptists. The boundary between legitimate and responsible persuasion and illegitimate and irresponsible pressure may not be easy to discern, but the Anabaptist commitment to religious liberty and freedom of conscience should make us sensitive to this issue and alert to abusive behavior.

- Ethical evangelism means friendship without strings attached. As mentioned earlier, most people become followers of Jesus because of the testimony (in word and deed) of their friends or family. Strategies, programs, and events play only subsidiary roles. This is often designated "friendship evangelism." With their emphasis on community, neo-Anabaptists naturally warm to this understanding of evangelism and endorse the attractive power of friendship and distinctive lifestyles. However, the term carries with it significant dangers, not least that friendship can be manipulative if the motivation for becoming a "friend" is to evangelize others.

- Ethical evangelism means sensitivity without compromise. The gospel needs to be translated and enculturated so that it makes sense to people, relates to their felt needs and aspirations, and addresses relevant issues. We need to find attractive words, images, and approaches. But it also challenges cultural norms and priorities, raises questions that people may not be asking, and presents fresh possibilities. Anabaptism has frequently been associated with countercultural witness, sometimes to the detriment of being culturally attuned, so this tradition may challenge us to avoid any watering down of the demands of the gospel.

- Ethical evangelism means humbly acknowledging that we cannot answer every question and are still discovering more about following Jesus. It means coming alongside others, learning from and with them, sharing what we know and believe, inviting and pondering their insights, and being open to fresh perspectives. A classic biblical example of "two-way" evangelism is Peter's encounter with Cornelius (Acts 10:1–11:18). This "God-fearing" Gentile was converted, but Peter's understanding of God and God's mission was also transformed, as subsequently was the church in Jerusalem. Peter discovered, much to his surprise, that God had already been at work in Cornelius's home long before he arrived.

None of this, though, implies that evangelism will gain much traction without the authentic witness of individuals and communities. This witness, in word and deed, will need to be gentle, gracious, winsome, respectful, and patient. Our tone of voice and attitudes are as crucial as anything we say as we bear witness in a multifaith, secular, and postsecular society as a minority community with a strange story to tell. But opportunities to tell this story are most likely to arise in contexts of friendship and partnership, in local neighborhoods and in shared projects, where followers of Jesus seek the common good (shalom) of a community rather than attempt to impose their agenda.[10] And Christian communities whose behavior provokes others to ask questions may be more missionally effective in post-Christendom than churches that are intent on giving out answers.

PEACE WITNESS

In contrast with what I heard from some North American Mennonites who expressed concern that advocating peace might discourage others from joining their churches, I have not encountered any such fear among British neo-Anabaptists. On the contrary, a commitment to nonviolence and active peacemaking might be the kinds of convictions and activities that provoke questions and invite others to explore a faith that inspires such beliefs and practices.

Like many others, I am not convinced that the term *pacifism* is at all helpful in this context. Although it is the traditional way of designating the stance of the Anabaptists and other historic peace churches, it conveys a notion of passivity. Because many critics associate pacifism with nonresistance, withdrawal, and lack of concern for justice or others beyond the pacifist community, this is unhelpful. Indeed, as was acknowledged in *The Naked Anabaptist*, "Anabaptists through the centuries have been guilty of passivity in the face of injustice, of disengagement from society, of confusing 'non-violence' with 'non-resistance,' of failing to move beyond opposition to war towards finding alternatives, of irresponsible idealism and otherworldly forms of spirituality."[11] Many Anabaptists today, however, are committed to a more proactive approach. This has meant exploring ways of pursuing justice through nonviolent and creative means, such as involvement in restorative justice, deploying peacemaking teams in areas of conflict, campaigning against the arms trade, exploring the malign legacies of colonialism, and many other initiatives. Once again, my colleague Noel Moules has coined an appropriate term, *shalom activism*, to convey this shift in perspective.

Neo-Anabaptist communities in post-Christendom may or may not be committed to absolute pacifism, as recent conversations have confirmed, but all of them will be concerned to pursue justice peacefully in their localities and beyond. In a deeply conflicted society and world, individuals and communities have multiple opportunities to engage in active peacemaking, so choices will need to be made in light of limited time and resources. Some examples were introduced in *The Naked Anabaptist* and need not be rehearsed here.[12] Many other examples can be found in Mennonite literature. Chapters 8 and 9 in this book introduce neo-Anabaptist mission initiatives that focus on active peacemaking in contested spaces. Here, I simply offer further examples of initiatives in which neo-Anabaptists are or may be involved.

One of these is the practice of restorative justice. This term was coined in the 1970s to describe a way of responding to criminal offending that concentrates on relational, emotional, and material repair rather than on conviction and punishment. It seeks to repair the harm that has been suffered and to do this, where possible, by actively involving the affected parties in mutual dialogue and decision-making about their needs and obligations. A restorative justice process brings together a victim and an offender in a facilitated face-to-face meeting to discuss the harm done. Restorative processes hold offenders accountable for their actions, help them understand the impact of their behavior, and offer them an opportunity to take responsibility and to make amends. They give victims a chance to tell offenders about the impact of their behavior and to receive answers and an apology. Restorative justice represents a "third way" between retribution and rehabilitation. Victims often find it helpful, and it has been shown to result in a substantial reduction in rates of reoffending.[13]

Restorative justice has become familiar in the UK and many other nations. It operates not only in the criminal justice system, but in community policing, education, human rights advocacy, environmental debates, workplace disputes, military disciplinary procedures, family mediation, and peacemaking initiatives. It influences social work, the probation service, schools, and prisons. It has been especially prevalent in New Zealand, where lessons have been learned from traditional Māori practices, and the first university chair in restorative

justice was established at the Victoria University of Welling-
ton. The first occupant of this chair was Christopher Marshall,
a member of the Anabaptist Association of Australia and New
Zealand, whose book *All Things Reconciled* commends the
practice of restorative justice to Christians concerned about
peacemaking in society.[14] An earlier book, *Compassionate
Justice*, offers an interdisciplinary study of the parables of the
good Samaritan and the prodigal son in relation to restorative
justice.[15] Marshall's involvement in this area of peacemaking
is one of several significant Anabaptist contributions to the
development of the principles and practices of restorative justice. A seminal work is *Changing Lenses* by American Mennonite Howard Zehr, first published in 1990.[16] And North
American Mennonites developed the Victim Offender Reconciliation Program, now operating under the auspices of the
Community Justice Center.[17]

The principles and practices of restorative justice embody
an Anabaptist approach to pursuing justice and responding to
the needs of victims (and offenders) in ways that are nonviolent
and encourage reconciliation and renewed relationships.
Restorative justice meetings can be understood as a missional
application of the principle of mutual accountability. This is a
form of peacemaking in which I have been involved for many
years. It is not a panacea, the outcome of the process is always
uncertain, and it is very poorly resourced compared with puni-
tive approaches to criminality, but it can be transformative.

A second form of peacemaking that Anabaptists have long
engaged is in forging relationships with members of other
faith communities. The writings of some early Anabaptists
indicate that their advocacy of religious liberty was not limited
to Christians who disagreed with each other but was intended
to include Jews, Muslims, and any others. Neo-Anabaptists

in plural post-Christendom contexts have opportunities to move far beyond what must have been a somewhat theoretical commitment in the European heartlands in the sixteenth century. The 2021 UK census, noted earlier, revealed not only a continuing decline of those who self-identify as Christians and a significant increase in those who declare that they have no religion, but also growth in the strength of other religious communities.[18]

Until relatively recently, Christians in Western nations rarely encountered members of other religious communities firsthand. Our perception of these other faiths and those who practiced them were largely shaped by travelogues, missionary accounts, and academic courses that introduced systems but failed to penetrate below the surface to the complex history, spirituality, and cultures of these religions. Conversations I have had in recent years with older church members have revealed ignorance, fear, stereotyping, and sometimes overt racism. Although we have Muslim, Buddhist, Hindu, and Sikh neighbors, work colleagues, doctors, lawyers, business leaders, and politicians (among many other occupations and religious communities), there are relatively few contexts where inherited assumptions can be questioned. One of the difficulties is the notion of "tolerance" advocated in our supposedly secular society, which discourages any exploration of differences between religions and attempts to prevent conflict by avoiding any possibility of giving offense. But this avoidance of conflict is not true peace, and this kind of tolerance means regarding all religious convictions as equally insignificant. This may satisfy secularists, who prefer to lump all faith communities together, but it is unlikely to be robust enough in an increasingly post-secular society, and it already hinders authentic friendships and conversations that move beyond the superficial.

At the international level, some Anabaptist leaders have pioneered initiatives to meet representatives of other religious communities, engage in respectful conversation, learn from one another, explore partnership possibilities, and become friends. One of the best known of these is David W. Shenk, who engaged in lifelong relationships with Muslim colleagues and friends. Shenk found in Sufism a "redemptive analogy" in their yearning to know God and appreciated the Sufi commitment to peacemaking in his birth country of Somalia, where Muslims partnered with Mennonites in times of conflict. He also collaborated with a Sunni Muslim colleague in Kenya, Badru Kateregga, to write *A Muslim and Christian in Dialogue*,[19] in which the two authors presented their views honestly and graciously, without polemics or attempting to interpret what the other had written. Shenk demonstrated that Christians and Muslims could be friends and cooperate together without denying the differences between their beliefs. Another North American Mennonite contribution is Gordon Nickel's book *Peaceful Witness among Muslims*, which draws on the peacemaking heritage of the Anabaptist tradition to outline ways of sharing the gospel in peaceful ways with Muslims.[20]

In a context of serious interreligious tension and conflict, Indonesian Mennonite Paulus Widjaja has engaged in courageous and creative efforts to build links with the Muslim community. As the director of the Center for the Study and Promotion of Peace at Duta Wacana Christian University, he trains Christians, Muslims, Hindus, and others in conflict transformation. He rejects the notion of mere coexistence or anemic tolerance, arguing for what he calls "pro-existence," mutual support, and a "dialogue of life," rather than just conversations.[21]

Anabaptists will also be eager to explore peace traditions in other religions and to find peacemakers in other faith communities, both to learn from them and to make common cause where appropriate. I have learned much from the book *Not in God's Name* by Jonathan Sacks, former chief rabbi of the United Hebrew Congregations of the Commonwealth. His book explores the often conflictual interrelationship between the three Abrahamic faiths.[22] Peaceful Borders, which is introduced in chapter 9, offers a grassroots example of peace-seeking Muslims and Christians working together, both employed by the Anabaptist Mennonite Network.

But there are many opportunities at a local level to move beyond "tolerance" and to form friendships and partnerships. These do not require us to compromise what we believe or to pretend we agree on everything, but they do require us to speak and act graciously, to listen carefully, to be open to fresh insights, to explore common concerns, and to welcome opportunities for partnership. Younger Christians, more at home in a plural culture, may much more easily forge friendships with members of other faith communities, but many will have imbibed the insipid secular notion of tolerance and so may be reluctant to engage in conversations about beliefs and practices. Perhaps neo-Anabaptist communities can model and advocate the much more robust and respectful practice of religious liberty.

Many of Urban Expression's mission partners live in multifaith neighborhoods and have engaged in various ways with members of other faiths. Often, the starting point has simply been conversations in shops or parks, at the school gate, or many other local meeting places. As friendships form, invitations to shared meals may follow. In some situations, conversations reveal shared concerns about local issues, such as drug dealing on the streets, racial injustice, or poor-quality housing, and partnerships emerge that can campaign for change or challenge local authorities to take action. It has been encouraging in recent years to hear of more and more initiatives involving churches and mosques offering mutual support and working together for the good of local neighborhoods. Neo-Anabaptist communities will likely want to participate in such initiatives and to explore ways of building friendships with members of other faith communities as a further expression of peaceful witness.

Friendships and partnerships with members of other faith communities are also, of course, expressions of witness in a post-Christendom and postcolonial context. In Western societies where even those with only a nominal Christian commitment make up less than half the population, Christian communities will need to learn how to act, speak, and think as one minority community among others. Neo-Anabaptists, as heirs of a marginalized tradition, should be better placed than many to embrace this stance and welcome the opportunities this context offers for witness that is no longer compromised by unhelpful assumptions and power dynamics. And this applies also to relationships with churches that are largely comprised of and led by Christians from the Majority World, whose presence in Western societies is already significant and has the potential to be a missional game-changer. Just as Western missionaries needed to adjust to the cultures where they found themselves in Africa and Asia, so Majority World Christians will need to learn how to engage with their secularized Western context. Conversations with Western followers of Jesus, such as those currently underway between the Zimbabwean Brethren in Christ churches in the UK and members of the Anabaptist Mennonite Network, can be helpful as long as there is postcolonial sensitivity, mutual respect, and two-way learning.[23]

EQUIPPING WITNESSES AND PEACEMAKERS

Whatever forms of peaceful witness neo-Anabaptist communities advocate, we will likely need to access or provide opportunities for training and reflection. While numerous missional training courses are available in the UK, few of these wrestle with the implications of post-Christendom, and fewer still focus on peacemaking. The Crucible course, run by Urban Expression in partnership with other agencies, is one exception.[24] This Anabaptist-oriented course, which since 2005 has equipped several hundred people, is deeply rooted in a *missio Dei* understanding of mission and includes modules entitled "After Christendom" and "Restoring Hope" (the latter explores aspects of peacemaking). Another UK initiative, one which owes much to North American Mennonite expertise, is the training offered by Bridge Builders on conflict transformation within congregations.[25]

A resource many of us have found helpful is a short booklet by Alan Kreider and Eleanor Kreider, published by the Anabaptist Network, entitled *Becoming a Peace Church*. The network has since developed a course to accompany this booklet, which can be accessed on its website.[26] The Kreiders provide biblical, historical, and theological foundations for churches to consider before offering practical guidance on such topics as developing the reflexes of peacemakers, the disciplines of peacemaking, the attitudes of peacemakers, and the skills of peacemakers. They then explore the implications of peacemaking for worship, work, war, and witness, concluding with some suggestions for how churches can pray for peace. Churches aspiring to be "peace churches" will also be attentive to the stories that are shared and, especially, the songs they sing, knowing that hymnody powerfully shapes our theology. The material in this booklet was expanded into a book, coauthored with Paulus Widjaja.[27] Much of this material is also integrated into a module, "Biblical and Practical Peacemaking," offered by the Centre for Anabaptist Studies each year.

An earlier chapter mentioned the Black Light course, which I organize in partnership with a Caribbean colleague, Les Isaac. We first taught this course in 1997 and recently revamped it and offered it online in light of heightened concerns about racial injustice after the murder of George Floyd in 2020. The course is a small contribution to peacemaking, enabling Black and White Christians to learn together from the Bible, history, and their own experiences, and to challenge all expressions of colonialism, racism, and white supremacy. An explicitly Anabaptist resource on peacemaking in relation to racism is the remarkable book by Osheta Moore, *Dear White Peacemakers*, set in her American context, but with poignant stories, biblical and theological reflections, practical guidance, and moving personal testimony that are not limited to that context.[28] Moore advocates and exemplifies a gracious and courageous expression of "shalom activism."

Talking about issues of peace and justice is still problematic in many churches, for fear of upsetting those who hold different views. But treating these issues as taboo or merely matters of personal opinion surely diminishes their significance. I recall a conversation many years ago with the leader of a network of churches who refused to consider exploring peace issues so as to avoid conflict or division in his churches, but who had endorsed the decisions of some congregations to split over the style and components of corporate worship. I was not persuaded by his priorities. If neo-Anabaptist communities subscribe to the seventh core conviction of the Anabaptist Mennonite Network, which insists that "peace is at the heart of the gospel," we are likely to explore ways to talk about peace and justice, equip each other for peaceful witness, reflect on our missional activities together, and gladly identify ourselves as peace churches. And we may conclude that our commitment to nonviolent peacemaking is more likely to attract than deter others in a culture that desperately needs to find ways of living peacefully together.

Section II

COMMON PRACTICES IN ACTION

In this section, three of my colleagues introduce initiatives they have taken over the past few years in partnership with the Anabaptist Mennonite Network. They have all been inspired by the Anabaptist vision, and their initiatives reflect this. Some of the initial and ongoing funding for these initiatives has been provided by the network, and the trustees provide support and accountability.

All three of my colleagues have also been deeply involved alongside me in Urban Expression, referenced in earlier chapters. As an Anabaptist-oriented mission agency, Urban Expression has been a seedbed for these further initiatives.

As you read these chapters, you will find echoes of the network's core convictions that were explored in *The Naked Anabaptist* and examples of the common practices examined in the first section of this book.

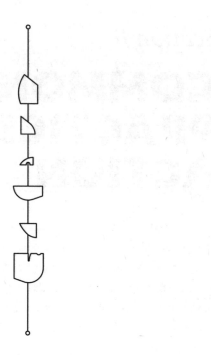

7

INCARNATE

Alexandra Ellish

HIDDEN TREASURE?

In the closing session of the Anabaptist Mennonite Network's March 2020 gathering to consider the case for church planting, one young man passionately urged those present: "It is as if you have this treasure; gold and riches in a chest. Do you not know how valuable that treasure is? Do you not perceive what you have that you could share?" The weekend gathering had been an opportunity to discern with a group of practitioners, theologians, and committed friends what the future might hold for the newly formed network. The Anabaptist Mennonite Network had been created by merger of the Anabaptist Network and the London Mennonite Trust earlier in the year, and church planting was one of the first strategic priorities that the network had gathered to discuss.

Church planting today looks materially different from five centuries ago when it was practiced by the early Anabaptists. At least in most places in Western Europe and North America, Christians are unlikely to face the persecution and suffering experienced by our Anabaptist forebears. Critics continue to question whether church planting is an unnecessary dilution of limited resources today, a risky endeavor with unknown outcomes, or even sectarian, but this controversial practice remains essential in our post-Christendom context. In recent years, we have witnessed growing momentum and greater creativity in this practice as churches from various traditions grapple with the challenge of engaging with a wider range of people in the changing contexts and complex cultures of the United Kingdom and Western Europe.[1]

I am convinced that the Anabaptist vision, particularly articulated in a UK context by the core convictions and common practices of the Anabaptist Mennonite Network (see appendices 1 and 2), offers inspiration and a rich resource for church planting and reimagining the nature and purpose of the Christian communities.

ANABAPTISTS IN THE UK

The Anabaptist Mennonite Network has its roots in the London Mennonite Centre, which was founded in 1953 and engaged in teaching and peace witness. This included offering welcome through a student residence, where, in a time of open racial hostility, North American Mennonite mission workers lived alongside Christians from across the world. Instead of setting up a new denomination, which might have threatened or been considered competition to local churches, they decided that the Mennonites would offer resources and insights from the Anabaptist-Mennonite tradition to Christians in other traditions. Although there were no attempts to plant churches, a Mennonite church emerged organically from the community of the London Mennonite Centre, but this closed in 2013 after several difficult years. The Anabaptist Network, formed in 1991, adopted the same policy of not planting churches but instead offering resources and building relationships with Christians inspired by the Anabaptist vision.

Nearly ten years ago, I spent some time working for the network, building relationships with younger adults who were interested in "anabaptisty" values—especially active peacemaking and reconciliation. I had countless cups of coffee and fascinating conversations with passionate, justice-seeking Jesus followers and activists. Many of them were working out their calling to be peacemakers through their professional work for organizations committed to the environment, debt relief, local and international peacemaking, and mediation. These young adults were not looking for a connection to a network or resources on Anabaptism, but they *were* looking for living, breathing communities of faith where they could see the Anabaptist values and convictions of earlier radical nonconformist communities worked out in the UK in the twenty-first century. I was frequently asked, "Where can I be part of this kind of community?" I had to admit that I had only a very limited number of suggestions.

There are currently no Anabaptist-Mennonite denominations active in the UK, although a number of local churches in membership with other denominations have also affiliated to the Anabaptist Mennonite Network. Currently, the two Bruderhof communities[2] and one largely Portuguese-speaking Mennonite church in Eastbourne are the only explicitly Anabaptist churches in the UK. The Brethren in Christ Church[3] has several small and mostly Zimbabwean congregations, which draw on Anabaptist, Wesleyan, evangelical, and Pietist traditions. There are also study groups and occasional gatherings of people connected with the network, but these are scattered across the UK in small numbers.

The sense that we could no longer ignore the question about the validity of Anabaptist church planting was the impetus for the March 2020 gathering to explore whether the "no church planting" policy was still serving the aims of the kingdom or whether it was time to reconsider and prioritize church planting. While the core convictions of what was then the Anabaptist Network had been formulated over twenty years earlier, the emergence of twelve common practices, which grounded the core convictions in real-life communities trying to work out how to live out those convictions, was an important milestone on the journey toward wondering about whether the network could provide companionship, support, and funding for people dreaming about forming new communities.

CHURCH PLANTING IN CONTEXT

During the past thirty-five years, various church planting campaigns and initiatives have been sponsored by denominations or mission agencies. The 1990s were declared a "Decade of Evangelism," and a major church planting campaign was initiated under the auspices of Challenge 2000, supported by most of the main denominations. This campaign had mixed success, and much of the church planting activity took place in more middle-class and affluent areas, neglecting and ignoring less desirable urban and marginalized communities. While the campaign fell well short of its goal to plant twenty thousand new churches by the year 2000, it was not a wholesale failure. Many churches were planted, and those who reflected on these initiatives at the end of the 1990s noted a number of encouraging lessons, including increased respect and mutual encouragement between denominations and a greater desire for collaboration and partnership.

From the late 1990s, the language around planting new forms of Christian communities was changing. Pioneers and those who supported them were wrestling with the interplay of church and mission, asking what kinds of communities should be planted, and how they should be planted. This conversation included phrases like "emerging church" and "fresh expressions of church," and stimulated creative experimentation with alternative forms of worship and community.

Urban Expression was founded in 1997 by Stuart Murray Williams and Jim and Juliet Kilpin as a grassroots church planting mission network committed to living in and discovering God in marginalized and deprived urban communities. This was, in part, a protest against the mostly homogenous church planting that had characterized the 1990s. Most new churches (except those planted within specific ethnic groups) looked very much like each other, and even the more experimental ones were mostly in more affluent and suburban neighborhoods. The values and commitments of Urban Expression[4] resonate deeply with those who join as mission partners and teams, whose initiatives range in size and character from social enterprises and missional communities to table churches and retreat homes. After completing my studies at the International Baptist Theological Seminary in Prague, I was ordained in the Baptist Union of Great Britain in 2009. I have been part of the Urban Expression community and engaged in urban mission and ministry in London for nearly fifteen years as a mission partner and coordinator. Urban Expression is not an explicitly Anabaptist church planting network, but the Anabaptist vision is evident in our values and commitments.

For some pioneers, community activists, and leaders (ordained and otherwise) *church planting* is an uncomfortable term. Because of our previous experiences, *church* has a wide range of meanings, expressions, and connotations. People can bring all sorts of assumptions about what church planting means when we talk about it! Likewise, the word *pioneer* conjures for some people images of swashbuckling explorers, or even more negatively the injustices of colonialism or domination. In this chapter, I use *church planting* to describe the patient work of grassroots relationship building and community engagement in the hope of giving birth to a new Christian community. These new communities might take root in any number of contexts, in various formats, shapes, or sizes. What makes it *church planting* is that there is a new or emerging Christian community that was not there before. I have not found a suitable replacement for *pioneer* to denote those who seek to plant and nurture these new communities, so I will stick with this term.

AS SMALL AS MUSTARD SEEDS

That March 2020 gathering inspired several efforts to further explore the question of church planting. The Anabaptist Mennonite Network has gathered resources for Christian communities already connected to the network to help them explore their distinctive Anabaptist identity alongside other communities in a yearlong "learning journey." One of the participants suggested forming a dispersed intentional Anabaptist community with a shared rule of life. Most significantly, after a period of discernment following that March weekend, the network made the exciting decision to prioritize church planting as a key project and area of development. The Incarnate initiative was born, and I was invited to chair its steering group.[5]

In May 2021, the Anabaptist Mennonite Network appointed Barney Barron and Lynsey Heslegrave as catalyst/coaches to support pioneers and those exploring new expressions of church that were drawing explicitly on the Anabaptist tradition. Like seed-saving gardeners, pioneers are gathering the heirloom seeds from earlier expressions of Anabaptist life and mission to cultivate new life. Let the planting begin!

Incarnate aims to seed, resource, and support new shapes and forms of Christian community inspired by the Anabaptist story and tradition. The core convictions of the network explored in *The Naked Anabaptist* as well as the common practices highlighted in the first section of this book are both a guiding light and a touchstone, providing inspiration and deeply held values to guide pioneers. Incarnate insists that it will be defined not "by doctrinal issues but by a passion for living out Anabaptist values through creating new Christian communities in a post-Christendom world."[6]

At the first gathering of Anabaptist church planters and pioneers in September 2022, the parable of the mustard seed, which appears in all three synoptic Gospels (Matthew 13:31–32; Mark 4:30–32; Luke 13:18–19), was a recurring theme that bubbled to the surface from speakers' presentations, Godly Play–inspired reflections,[7] and informal conversations. This was not planned—it emerged spontaneously and clearly as a meaningful story for the conference. This parable resonated with the practitioners who had gathered together because it speaks to the fragility of what they are trying to do—starting with very small seeds and waiting, hoping for growth. Interestingly, although the biblical texts call it a tree, most mustard seed varieties grow into low bushes or shrubs, which can spread extensively across a wide area of ground. In some places they are even considered weeds! This image of a stubborn plant, spreading in small but determined ways across different terrains, even providing nourishment and sanctuary to other creatures, continues to delight and inspire us.

CREATIVITY AND COMMUNITY

The Incarnate initiative is an experiment, a sandpit for exploration, through which the Anabaptist Mennonite Network wants to facilitate a flexible and creative approach to Anabaptist church planting. These new expressions of church will look different according to their contexts, and there is no restriction on their geographic, cultural, or socioeconomic settings. It may be that an Anabaptist expression of church will emerge from a group of people serving a marginalized subculture or particular people group. A group of peacemakers might gather around a specific injustice, and an expression of community might emerge from their commitment to Jesus the Prince of Peace. Our hope is that a small "community of communities" might emerge so that these communities can learn together, journey together, pray for, and support each other in their calling to a specific mission.

Creativity is a necessary posture for approaching church planting in the twenty-first century. Familiar forms of church are struggling to engage with most people, and there is a diversity of cultures and subcultures in Britain today. This requires contextual sensitivity and awareness, imagination, and resilience. The common practices will hopefully provide a helpful starting point for Anabaptist church planters, but they will have to apply and interpret these for their own contexts. Contemporary church planters share this posture with their Anabaptist forebears—early Anabaptists were experimenters and adventurers, melding together practices to nurture new communities that took seriously both discipleship and mission.

Eating together has always been an important part of community formation and relationship building, and a number of Incarnate pioneers center the table in their community life. SoulSpace Belfast has even named their gathering The Table.

Eating together symbolizes welcome, acceptance, hospitality, and inclusion. Shared meals can be a helpful container for intergenerational relationship building, where young and old can easily join in. For communities that experiment with the potluck approach, combining our resources to create a shared feast is an eschatological vision of reconciliation for all people and all creation.

Communities meeting primarily around the table might also find that other common practices, such as being multivoiced, exercising shared leadership, and engaging in consensual decision-making, are easier to practice together. This may also be how people in communities offer each other mutual aid. However, if our "peace meals" are to be places of true inclusion and welcome, we will need to pay attention to issues of inequality, cultural norms, and social knowledge about what to do and how to do it when inviting people to our tables. At their heart, shared meals can be a creative, countercultural expression of love, peace, restoration, hope, and friendship across diversity and difference—the kin-dom of God here and now.

COUNTERING ISOLATION

One of the biggest challenges that pioneers and innovators face is the loneliness of setting out, moving beyond known traditions and patterns to risk trying new things. Pioneers are often misunderstood, and starting something from scratch has unique challenges that inherited churches do not face. Pioneers often do not have access to funding, resources, and established systems of support and accountability. Pioneers (through necessity or intention) are frequently bivocational, juggling home, work, and ministry responsibilities. Pioneering is more often a marathon, not a sprint. Building relationships takes time and commitment, and the "results" are frequently undramatic to an outside observer. Some pioneers are working on their own, without the support of a partner, family, or nearby relatives. Particularly when working in marginalized neighborhoods, in this time of volatility and economic pressure, these factors can make pioneering very challenging and lonely.

Funding the Incarnate catalyst/coaches is one way of mitigating loneliness. Barney Barron and Lynsey Heslegrave, the catalyst/coaches deployed by the Anabaptist Mennonite Network, support pioneers by building connections, initially through one-to-one conversations, and then gathering small groups of people, online and in person, to exchange ideas, build community, pray for, and encourage each other. Barney and Lynsey are based in different parts of the UK, helping them build relationships across a wider area. While technology provides fantastic opportunities for meeting people from diverse geographic areas, Barney and Lynsey prioritize visiting pioneers to increase their understanding of the contexts where pioneers are operating, what they have already been doing, and what support is needed to nurture their mustard seed of a dream. The annual Incarnate house party provides a relaxed, informal environment to explore questions, share frustrations, and celebrate learning and achievements.

Pioneers and those experimenting with new ways of forming community also need examples and stories from those who have gone before them. Sharing stories and experiences as co-learners is an important element of the Incarnate community. The catalyst/coaches also serve to give permission for people, particularly women, who might have experiences of being ignored, undermined, or underappreciated in previous church contexts. Giving permission for people to try something without fear of failure in a context where the mainstream church seems to be functioning with a scarcity, fear-based mindset is a joyful and liberating part of the work of the Incarnate initiative.

From my conversations with Barney and Lynsey, it is clear that pioneers most value the community of fellow travelers and practitioners that Incarnate seeks to bring together. The early Anabaptists were committed to being a community of disciples who practiced mutual accountability and valued truth-telling. In our time, when we are frequently faced with misinformation, fake news, and online bickering, the Anabaptist common practices of truth-telling and mutual accountability might be restorative, foster mutuality, and lead to deeper relationships.

ADVENTURES IN ANABAPTIST CHURCH PLANTING

At the time of this writing, the Incarnate project is nearly two years old, so it is still early days. But there are encouraging signs of new life. It is important to protect these fledgling expressions from the heat and light of a full beam of attention, so these stories are not drawn out in detail but hopefully still illustrate some of what is emerging.

SoulSpace Belfast is among the first of these emerging expressions that identifies as an Anabaptist-inspired community. SoulSpace Belfast is an alternative community that draws on Celtic and Anabaptist spiritualities within the postconflict context of Northern Ireland. Their values are focusing on Jesus, social justice, peacebuilding, generosity, hospitality, and a desire to create community. Karen Sethuraman's chapter in this book tells the story in richer detail. Through friendship and seizing opportunities for mutual learning, SoulSpace Bristol has since emerged, drawing on the experience of the Belfast community, with whom they share their name.

SoulSpace Bristol[8] is a gathering of Jesus-followers led by Rachel Haig, a Baptist minister and community center manager. This community grew out of Rachel's vision of creating a space for people who want to follow Jesus. With a small team of leaders, she laid the foundation for a community that would take seriously the Anabaptist story, as well as drawing on the resources offered by Godly Play and a deep commitment to be incarnationally rooted in a local neighborhood. SoulSpace Bristol meets twice a month in a community center to share food and pursue Jesus-centered welcome. Belonging is a core value of SoulSpace Bristol, and this is articulated through a prayer litany used every time they meet together.[9]

Through conversations in the core group, SoulSpace Bristol has created a set of values which form the basis for their community life. Anabaptist core convictions are clearly discernible in these eight values (which SoulSpace Belfast has also adopted and which Karen Sethuraman lists in the next chapter). These include the centrality of being Jesus followers, living as an egalitarian community committed to peacemaking (with all of creation), and practices of simplicity and generosity.

SoulSpace Bristol is an emerging community that has already had to traverse a deep ravine of the unexpected death of a key community member at the very start of their journey, which their community is still processing. Rachel is honest about the challenges of setting out for an unknown destination. However, the partnership with SoulSpace Belfast offers mutual support and companionship for the road, and Rachel is confident that many new opportunities lie ahead.

Based in Looe, Cornwall, Cimarron is an emerging Christian community led by Barney Barron. The group started in 2019 as a few new arrivals into the area were looking for a church but were not drawn to any of the established churches.

A number of group members had Baptist backgrounds, and during the COVID-19 lockdown they studied *The Naked Anabaptist*. The core convictions resonated with the group, particularly those relating to multivoiced worship and the co-creation of spaces to deepen relationship with each other and with God. They meet weekly on Sundays (ironically, for a pioneering community, the most traditional day to meet). The first hour of their time together is given over to a shared meal to which everyone is invited to contribute (if it is a beautiful day in Cornwall, you have to have a barbecue!). The second hour follows a pattern that they hold to lightly: exploring God through sung worship; exploring God through nature; exploring God through the Word; exploring God through food/ the table. On the fifth Sunday, they do something social, and between weekly gatherings, members are encouraged to spend informal, unhurried time together—going for walks, coffees, or heading to the pub.

The Anabaptist Mennonite Network core convictions have been a formative source of inspiration for Barney, who has observed that the group's values have drawn people into the church and have also been a guide to their communal life. At the moment, there is no formal leadership team, but as the community grows and wants to maintain their multivoiced approach, it might be necessary to develop a core team to help share oversight of the church.

Finally, Themba Ndlovu, a leader in the Brethren in Christ Church, is enthusiastic about the possibilities and relationships which might develop through the Incarnate project. The eleven churches that constitute the BICC in the UK are increasingly self-identifying as Anabaptist. Unlike the other emerging communities, the BICC is an established denomination, but their Anabaptist convictions and commitment to church planting are leading to deepening relationships with Incarnate. For Themba, the importance of keeping Jesus as the central focus for faith, discipleship, and mission is a key factor. Themba sees parallels between the early Anabaptist gatherings and the BICC church planting model. Most BICC churches start organically with about five people meeting for conversation and Bible study. Themba emphasizes the importance of the church being in the community so people can disciple and encourage each other as well as support and minister to their neighbors. These groups of neighborhood-based Jesus followers can be "little lights" in their communities.

As a mostly Zimbabwean network of churches, the BICC is asking how they might become more multicultural and welcoming to those with no previous church experience, and how they can connect with the younger, second-generation Africans in their neighborhoods. There is potential for rich learning and collaboration on the journey toward becoming more multicultural communities of faith for many of those interested in church planting. It would be fantastic to see a number of multicultural church planting teams initiated through the Incarnate project.

FORMING COMMUNITY, NOT INSTITUTIONS

The model that most of the Incarnate initiatives are working with, consciously or not, is the "centered set" model, as opposed to the "bounded set" model. For bounded-set groups, there is clear delineation between those who are "in" and those who are "out." While bounded-set churches may say that everyone is welcome, specific membership criteria and expectations about correct behavior and beliefs must often be subscribed to before "outsiders" can be integrated into the community. Centered-set churches function with no boundaries, no insiders and outsiders. They understand themselves as a group of people who are moving at different speeds toward the center of their communal life, which is Christ. This model recognizes that people's faith journeys are not linear, and that belonging is defined not by conforming to particular beliefs or behaviors but by the direction of travel. Those closer to the center actively participate in the life and mission of the community and are committed to following Jesus.[10]

Although Anabaptist churches have traditionally operated as bounded-set churches, it may be that centered-set churches with strong core convictions but open edges are more contextually appropriate and missionally potent in post-Christendom societies. The Cimarron community is wrestling with this question. Do they require commitment to the Anabaptist core convictions, or can the core team hold to these convictions but have open edges in a centered-set approach?

There are many important questions about how a new community will identify itself and articulate its beliefs. How will they engage with the Anabaptist core convictions and common practices? Is it sufficient for the initial team or main leaders to subscribe to these values? Should these be communicated regularly and explicitly from the very beginning, or do they infuse everything that the community does and thus not require special attention? How are the core convictions held faithfully by a community, without inadvertently becoming a pseudo-statement of faith? There are other questions about how a group legally constitutes itself (or whether it should) and whether it is helpful, necessary, or desirable to set up structures up front or as things develop. Should pioneers register as charities and open bank accounts to provide the right legal framework from the beginning? Or is it better to wait and see?

Lynsey Heselgrave has reported that, for some of those with whom she engages, the lack of clear boundary lines, such as statements of faith and formal (and exclusive) membership criteria, is a key attraction of the Incarnate initiative. This raises questions about how we understand belonging and participation in emerging Anabaptist communities, what role accountability has in these communities, and how the practices of the early Anabaptists, such as mutual submission and communal discipleship, can be reimagined for today. As indicated in earlier chapters, communities will need to respond to these questions in their own contexts, but we hope that our catalyst/coaches will also help foster conversations between communities.

LOOKING BACK, LOOKING FORWARD

Might something emerge from any of these experiments? If we fail to take some risks, how can we respond when people ask us about community expressions of shalom and peacemaking? As there is no official Anabaptist denomination in the UK, how might these new communities connect with each other? Who will provide accountability for them? Many questions remain, but I am convinced of the clear need for the planting of new churches in the peace church tradition in the UK—particularly at this time of political and social turmoil, when there is a deep need for active nonviolence, reconciliation between hurting people and communities, and daily practices to sustain discipleship. The pandemic has offered us a fresh opportunity to reimagine Christian community with less power and privilege but deeper relationships and clearer commitment to the person of Jesus.

The early Anabaptists were passionate church planters, committed to establishing new churches instead of reforming existing ones. Today, some church planters are drawing inspiration from the Anabaptist tradition as they reflect on how to engage in culturally sensitive and contextually appropriate mission. Although the present-day and Radical Reformation contexts are separated by five hundred years of history and are very different, the Anabaptists emerged at a time of similar cultural and societal flux. They might offer us some insights into how we inhabit and witness to an alternative narrative to our dominant culture.

In a climate of fear and suspicion, Anabaptist communities can welcome people to tables of hospitality and reconciliation. In a time of isolation and loneliness, they can extend friendship and community, traveling companions on the journey of faithfully following Jesus. In a context of uncertainty and transition, Anabaptists today can learn from the experiences of their spiritual forebears, who often worked out their discipleship at the margins of society. As Incarnate pioneers set out courageously and joyfully into the unknown, my hope is that they will draw with gratitude on the treasures of the Anabaptist story. May those tiny mustard seeds grow roots and spread like persistent weeds—Jesus-following communities embedded in their neighborhoods and networks, stubbornly committed to the kingdom of God.

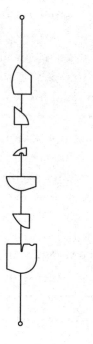

8

SOULSPACE BELFAST

Karen Sethuraman

The Anabaptist Mennonite Network has a vision to plant peace churches that make Jesus the center of their lives, have a commitment to intentional discipleship, and are mission focused. Chapter 7 introduced the Incarnate initiative that is pursuing this vision. SoulSpace Belfast is an early expression of this in a context where peace and reconciliation are desperately needed.

DIVISION, DECLINE, AND CHANGE

The real division of Ireland is not a line drawn on the map, but in the minds and hearts of its people.

John Hume, SDLP leader in Ireland and Nobel Peace Prize winner

The Irish political landscape is changing. Twenty-five years after the Good Friday Agreement, Northern Ireland continues to maintain peace and a certain level of stability. However, sectarian tensions and division remain. Decades of media reports exploring this complicated and complex situation have highlighted that, despite numerous attempts at an ongoing peace process, Catholics and Protestants remain fundamentally divided. This division is expressed not only through segregated church attendance but also in neighborhoods, schools, sports, social gatherings, and use of the Irish language.

Sociologists, historians, and theologians have all attempted to explain and engage with the sectarianism that is endemic to this society. Most conclude that religion is the source and stimulus of bigotry and parochialism. Religious affiliation informs nearly every aspect of life and defines many boundaries, not simply those that are clearly church-related. The clash of religious identities is a result of entrenched doctrinal positions and results in persistent sectarianism.

A recent *Life and Times* survey revealed that 80 percent of people in Northern Ireland claim to be spiritual, but less than 30 percent attend church. This would suggest that there are those who are disillusioned not necessarily with the Christian faith, but rather with the institution and organized religion. There are many reasons why people may find themselves outside the institution. Certainly, within my own context, where historically, Christianity "has shaped in powerful ways the island's cultures and languages as well as people's conception of what it means to be an individual, a family, a community, and a nation,"[1] church attendance is in rapid decline. Contributing factors include devastating revelations of historical institutional abuse; the mother and baby homes scandal, involving the appalling treatment of unwed mothers and their children in institutions run mostly by Catholic nuns; the role the church has played in the conflict; and a perceived inability to be relevant.[2]

It is in this context that SoulSpace Belfast was birthed.

EARLY QUESTIONS

I grew up in East Belfast, raised by a single mum. From an early age I attended a local Baptist church, and I am thankful for their input into my spiritual formation, particularly during my younger years. As a teenager, I recall being taught that women had no place at the leadership table and could not be ordained within the Irish Baptist tradition. This did not bother me much, at least not until I reached my late teens and felt a call into ministry life. Despite the lack of opportunities for women, I was encouraged to begin my theological training, which eventually led to my employment in a Baptist church. My ministry role at the time was to bridge the gap between the church and community, and to think of creative ways to integrate those outside the church walls into our church family. I confess I struggled with this.

After all, why do we feel that our mission is primarily to invite people to come into our churches? Is the measure of kingdom success based on the growth of our church? Are we really just about getting people "saved"? Such questions unsettled me. I also had wider questions regarding church and community: women in church leadership, faith and sexuality, racism, and sectarianism, as well as concerns about the limitations of the church in relation to peace and reconciliation, particularly in our divided context. Looking back, it was as if my theology and reality were disconnecting. Many describe such questioning as a form of faith deconstruction, and for me, this was certainly the beginning of a period of rethinking and examining, an unlearning and unpacking of my belief system. In addition to this, I repeatedly heard from people in the community, "I don't fit in church." Mind you, I was beginning to feel as though I did not fit either.

Together with a few others, my questioning spirit began to wonder whether it was possible to set up a home for people wearied by the institutional church. Or was the cultural chasm too wide? Eventually, fifteen years ago, I stepped out of institutional church and began a journey of unlearning, reinvention, and experimentation to provide a place of belonging for all. Over time, and with many mistakes, a template has evolved that enables our fledging community to engage with God and with people.

SOULSPACE: AN ALTERNATIVE COMMUNITY

It is often not so much the institutional Church or churches, but individuals who seek out the roots of spirituality: institutions as a rule follow where individuals have led.

The Irish Inter-Church Meeting, *The Dearest Freshness Deep Down Things*[3]

Our attempt to establish an authentic alternative community relevant to the Irish context flourished. This was launched initially as Down Community Church, because our spiritual rootedness began in County Down in Northern Ireland. The vision grew from the realization that for many people a more traditional form of church felt inaccessible and irrelevant. However, a few years into our journey, we realized that what we had planted followed the same format as the churches we had previously led, with our gatherings consisting of sermons, worship, and various programs.

We often reflect on those early years as "the years we got it wrong," as we found ourselves pandering too much to the expectations of religious people who tend to circulate among various churches. We were not exempt from this tendency, so we attracted many discontented Christians who belonged to other churches. They eventually left because we were too chaotic for them. If planting an alternative community has taught us anything, it is this: if you are looking for anything well-organized and structured, do not come here. However, this gave us the opportunity to start over afresh and to figure out what God wanted us to do.

CELTIC AND ANABAPTIST INFLUENCE

In our post-conflict context, we sought a spirituality that pre-dated the Reformation and could possibly help us avoid our modern tribal sectarian divisions. We recognized that some-times, in order to go forward, you have to go back, so we began retracing the ancient Celtic way. This has had a profound impact on the shaping, experience, and expression of our faith community. Our journey of rediscovery introduced us to Celtic saints such as Patrick, Bridget, Brendan, and Ita, and we even held a Celtic Christian retreat to the sites associated with Saint Patrick in the town of Downpatrick. We were able to share the gospel with those who participated in this spiritual experience.

During this season, the words of Jeremiah became import-ant to us: "Stand at the crossroads, and look, and ask for the ancient paths, where the good way lies; and walk in it, and find rest for your souls" (Jeremiah 6:16).

At that time, our team members all came from a Protestant evangelical background, so it was critical for us to embrace this journey of unlearning and relearning. We encountered the ancient practice of *lectio divina*; the art of icons, poetry, storytelling; the importance of embracing mystery and con-templation; and the benefits of a multivoiced community. Our journey helped us realize that our work is not a new, detached movement, but rather a reenvisioning of pre-Reformation faith, which we seek to apply within our Irish setting. As our community was growing, we acknowledged the need to find a wider network of pioneers involved in similar work to connect with for support and accountability.

We first met Stuart Murray Williams in 2012, and he shared the story of the early Anabaptists with us. The Anabaptists emerged during an era when the principle *cuius regio, eius religio* (the religion of the rulers must be the religion of their subjects) held sway. The Anabaptists dissented and made "a faith decision that directly confronted and challenged the social, religious, and even political status quo."[4] As a result, they found themselves outside of the institution, subsequently labeled the "unwanted and unloved stepchild of the church."[5] In brief, sixteenth-century Anabaptism is a story of spiritual refugees who were cast out but were determined to live out their deeply held and shared Anabaptist convictions. This required alternative communities. Discussing the spread and development of the early Anabaptists, historian C. Arnold Snyder describes their journey as moving from "genesis to exodus." In other words, as a result of severe persecution, this newly formed group of radicals were a people in search of their own "promised land—a place of refuge."[6]

We found ourselves identifying with the story of the Anabaptists and, in hearing it, felt a strong sense of coming home. Perhaps, like the Anabaptists, people in Ireland feel that the church has lost its way and refuse to settle for the status quo. Consequently, this has rendered them spiritual refugees. I have always been drawn to stories of people who feel they do not fit, especially in the church. Perhaps this is because it resonates with my own story, but what I have discovered throughout my ministry life is that many people who do not attend church are still deeply spiritual. Indeed, those who feel they "don't fit" in church may be no less spiritual than those who do.[7]

A COMMUNITY SURVEY

While embarking on our journey of discovering the story of the Celtic and Anabaptist ways, we also conducted a community survey to gauge how we might move forward. These are the three questions we asked and the answers we received:

What do you think are the current tensions in Northern Ireland? *Division. Sectarianism. Leadership vacuum: lack of direction in leadership and the Northern Ireland Assembly. Poverty. Increased racism. Paramilitarism involved in organized crime. Drugs. Behind the rest of UK with regards to women's rights. Polarizations of the tribes here. Lack of faith in authority. Difficulty dealing with our past/legacy issues. Conflicting historical stories and differing accounts of our story.*

Do you think faith communities have a part to play? *Faith is important, but religion is the cause of conflict here. There needs to be authenticity and willingness to take appropriate risks. Church needs to deal with its own "skeletons in the closet" in relation to clerical abuse, mother and baby homes, and so on. Faith has become toxic when mixed with politics—how do we challenge this? The Bible is often weaponized to justify political and ethnic stances on "For God and Ulster,"[8] exclusion of LGBT+ people in relation to equal marriage, and so on. Greater need for interchurch and interfaith partnership—the church is not very good at engaging with the "other." Time for the separation of church and state. Learn to handle difference well. Healing the past. Model reconciliation.*

What do you think are the solutions? *Humility and not arrogance. Embrace society with radical love. Engage with the issues "while being scared that we don't*

know the answer." Know that the answer is not always Jesus—
the teaching in Northern Ireland is still mainly focused on "get-
ting saved and how to get to heaven"—this needs to change.
Be willing to be misunderstood. Stand with the marginalized
and oppressed and create friendships with the "other." Talk
less, instead be present and listen. Create space for better
engagement and conversation. Be an alternative faith voice
that Northern Ireland so desperately needs.

Reflecting on this survey, we realized that our work must extend beyond our gathering to include the imperative to be agents of peace and reconciliation in the mending of our communities. Eventually, this led us to transition from Down Community Church into SoulSpace Community, a peace and reconciliation hub.

WHAT DO WE DO?

We seek to figure out what it means to love our neighbor in our communities and beyond. Our priority is simply to journey with people rather than provide programs, so institutional structure is not important to us. Our values are love, grace, acceptance, generosity, hospitality, creativity, influence, and risk. Our work is not a new way of living the spiritual life, but rather an endeavor to connect the old to the new, taking our example from Jesus, who was genius at loving people into change. The challenge for SoulSpace is to seek ways in our divided context to be peacemakers, voices of hope, grace, compassion, and peace, fueled by a determination to figure out what it truly means to live as neighbors with the "other."

We offer community chaplaincy, promote peace and reconciliation through various projects, develop partnerships with other peace and reconciliation hubs, champion public theology, and seek to train and support volunteers. We also have a gathering (both face-to-face and online) for people who feel they "don't fit" in church.

Recently, we were excited to hear from friends who have planted a SoulSpace community in Bristol.[9] We are delighted to partner with them, and they have given us permission to share their core values as an extension of our own:

- We will be a community of Jesus-centered followers.
- We will be a welcoming community that shares both laughter and tears together. Our community will be egalitarian, inclusive, and affirming.
- We will be a community that is open and exploring, where doubt is fine, and where listening to one another is valued.
- Our individual and corporate lifestyle will be one of hospitality, simplicity, and generosity.
- We will be committed to loving our neighbor in practical ways.
- We will pursue peace and be known as peacemakers.
- We will stand for social justice in our local communities, our country, and as far as possible, throughout the world.
- We will be committed to creation care and respect for the environment.

PEACE AND RECONCILIATION

SoulSpace seeks to join in with what already exists in our local community, and to be a Jesus people right in the middle of it all. If we believe that outward acts of social change and partnering with existing community development are defining aspects of the gospel, then we, as an alternative Irish spiritual community, want to offer a physical expression of what it means to identify with the kingdom of God here within our context. We feel that a significant part of our work going forward will be in peacebuilding and reconciliation projects, seeking to build bridges between communities.

Our work has taken place in various locations, including rural areas in South Down, as well as North and West Belfast. However, I recently spent several months conversing with friends of SoulSpace (as well as colleagues) about the way forward. One thing that kept emerging during our discussions, particularly with the folks connected to SoulSpace, was a desire to return to simple community. Down Community Church began in our living room in 2009, and a number of folks said how they missed those days—and I missed them too. I confess that, somewhere along this journey, we had lost sight of the original vision of simplicity and hospitality, so we decided to bring the gathering back to our living room; to bring people back to our home.

At the heart of our work was setting up a community chaplaincy, which has involved us getting deeply involved in ministry within local communities where drug culture, arranged gang fights, crime, paramilitary activities, poverty, and other social issues are prevalent. Our community chaplaincy model is heavily relational and time intensive, and includes being out on the streets, drinking endless coffees, and developing friendships. We have connected with so many people from all backgrounds and have had the privilege of conducting weddings, funerals, blessings, and invocations at community events.

Our involvement has led us over the years to work with local residents, community police officers, politicians, asylum seekers, and church and community groups. Some of the projects we have been involved in include partnering with a local residents' group in the improvement of their community, providing pastoral care, helping to establish a small community foodbank, and being present on the streets during a time of political and community unrest sparked by the Northern Ireland Protocol, when riots spilled into the streets. We have also participated in services involving many local church leaders and denominational representatives and a public march of witness for peace in the community.

Our aim is to champion social justice, so we have been involved in projects concerning gender equality, setting up a space for LGBT+ people of faith, racial equality, and interfaith work through our involvement on the Northern Ireland Interfaith Forum. The work of SoulSpace is becoming more widely known, resulting in invitations to speak at conferences concerning peace and reconciliation, and we have even been asked to contribute to the wider conversation about building a better future on the island of Ireland. This has included the honor of twice being asked to address the Committee for the Implementation of the Good Friday Agreement in the Irish Parliament. We have made international connections through the Mennonite Mission Network, and we are excited about opportunities for the cross-fertilization of ideas and resources.

OUR GATHERINGS

We have found our home with the Anabaptists and share their common practices: focusing on Jesus, social justice, peacebuilding, generosity, hospitality, and a desire to create community. SoulSpace is simply attempting to recover the Celtic and Anabaptist ways and retell them in a new language, presenting a different approach to worship, practices, and the Bible, without much church structure. SoulSpace does not begin with theological doctrinal positions; rather, we start with what we all have in common—our questions, fears, joys, challenges, ambitions, and so on. Presence, influence, relationship, story, and the recognition that everyone is made in the image of God are paramount to us. We seek to journey spiritually with people, taking them from where they are to the place God wants them to be, and we are not out to fix anybody.

Traditional church is largely passive, whereas at SoulSpace we have discovered that spiritual disciplines are very immersive and inclusive, and we have found them to be transformational. Our gathering is called The Table, and this is where much discussion, freedom to question, and the exchange of ideas take place. We gather once a month in a relaxed and informal setting, with extensive use of the visual (arts and icons), liturgy, storytelling, *lectio divina*, and a conversational teaching component that is dialogical and interactive. Our prayers have been both traditional and colloquial, offered in everyday language; we also make use of ancient prayers. The primary question for our community is not who is going to heaven and who is not, but rather, How can we be Jesus in our divided context? There is no upbeat high-energy music or slow ballad-type worship seeking to achieve an emotional setting to generate a response to faith, and no one turns up expecting the invitation to get "saved." Instead, we simply unite with a desire to encounter God. Even though our spiritual growth trajectories may vary dramatically, we experience God together as fellow travelers. However, it is the time and energy invested in relationships that has proved most significant.

One of the strongest emphases from voices within the Celtic and Anabaptist tradition is that of community. The importance of this practice is rooted in Scripture. The early church was notable for its devotion to fellowship and the quality of its common life (Acts 2:42–47). Over the years we have gathered in pubs, cafés, houses, community halls, and former church halls, as well as outside in nature, with the intention of living out the concept of *being* the church rather than *going* to church. Our vision is to build what the Irish call *trasnas* (which can be translated as "crossing")—seeking to cross our religious divides and build bridges to those far from God, extending to the forgotten, marginalized, and disillusioned.

As with every other organization, our work was somewhat hindered and recalibrated by the pandemic, especially as at the time we were embedded in community buildings, both former churches—one Presbyterian and the other Methodist. Even though we were unable to connect with people face-to-face, we stayed in touch virtually with our network of contacts by telephone and Zoom. However, during this season, our work was becoming more widely known and followed, so we conducted an online poll to gauge the interest in an online space for spiritual refugees. In all, 250 people responded: 92 percent said yes and 8 percent said no. Consequently, in 2022, we launched our online SoulSpace Community, and over 250 people have become members. We currently have a team of six contributors who lead our online group, and we have also started to gather at our "Virtual Table" for reflection, conversation, and prayer. This space has become an important vehicle for us to connect with people who are unable to join in our face-to-face gatherings.

I confess that this work is at times extremely difficult and challenging, and I have often thought about giving up. Stepping out of institutional church was not easy, and I refer to that particular season of my ministry life as my wilderness years, when I felt that everything was being stripped away. I felt a deep loneliness and encountered severe opposition that

I had never experienced before. Nothing prepared me for this journey. Churches have been our greatest critics, and during the early days I was told by church leaders not to plant a community in their neighborhood, nor to take any of their people with me. Leaders have refused to work with me. I have received telephone calls and emails telling me to pull out of events, and I have been warned to "tread carefully." Some have protested that I am not really ordained and have questioned my credentials and ordination, despite my accreditation with the Baptist Union of Great Britain. I have been branded a heretic and to this day still receive horrific ongoing abuse concerning my gender and my work. I know what it is to feel misrepresented, misunderstood, and misinterpreted, and I have often doubted whether I made the right decision to step out of the institution, rather than remaining in the safety of a church family.

Throughout our SoulSpace journey, there have been seasons of learning and unlearning, people coming and going, laughter and crying, pain and joy, team and no team, encouragement and discouragement, being ridiculed and cheered on, energy and exhaustion, achievements and many failures, and also times of wondering whether we will survive. However, God has been faithful, and we remain seized by a vision to set up a home for the spiritual refugees.

THE CHURCH IS CHANGING

Today, SoulSpace continues to grow and is beginning to influence church (and political) circles in Ireland, but even still, few seem to understand its crucial modus operandi. Similarly to the Anabaptists, our experiential and participatory approach has received much criticism, and we have experienced our own marginalization. But with the Irish no longer trusting institutions across all spheres of life and wearied by religion, SoulSpace will continue to deconstruct and reconstruct faith by intentionally creating anti-institutional structural forms.

We are not suggesting that Irish Christianity has no positive historical past, or that the configuration of Christianity required to address the Irish religious divide must be created from scratch. Neither are we, as some critics may suggest, "treating the disciplines of the church as outward clothing."[10] In fact, we are simply returning to the ancient faith and practices for Christian examples, particularly those which predate the Reformation. There is no more seminal understanding of our community than the belief that the presence of God is here and now. Anabaptism is centered on the life and ministry of Jesus; this approach invites us to leave out all the Catholic and Protestant jargon and instead simply focus on him. The Anabaptist Christocentric focus reminds us that Jesus took on our human culture and practices, becoming one of us, and participating in the local community life, making himself accessible. A literal translation of John 1:14 is "pitched his tent among us." *The Message* translation says that he "moved into the neighborhood." My hope is that we can avoid the prevalent tendency in the Irish churches to invest too much energy on whose doctrine is right, and rather unite around the desire to be Jesus in our communities.

Theological debate is an ongoing task for the church in any era, and it is an essential activity for anyone who wishes to engage in effective peacebuilding in Ireland. But without an intentional unifying framework of reconciliation that specifically tackles the Catholic and Protestant dichotomy, there is a real danger that what is planted will duplicate what already exists—the mistake we made in the early years as a community. Going forward, a possible solution may be found in creating intentional Anabaptist spiritual communities, such as SoulSpace. Historian Walter Klaassen describes the Anabaptist movement as neither Catholic nor Protestant, and in many ways it represents the best of both traditions. He writes that the Anabaptists' desire to reform the church caused them to "consciously and deliberately return to primitive models for guidance; that is back to the roots of Christianity in the New Testament."[11] The Anabaptist vision was for ecclesial reconstruction rather than institutional reform.

From the onset, Anabaptist ecclesiology is a reminder that God's mission extends beyond the boundaries of the institutions. The bold prophetic voices of the early Anabaptists, calling out the corruption in the institution and the state in their generation, challenge the contemporary church to take a similar stand. Turning a blind eye and remaining silent is bound to damage Christian witness.

Perhaps we must face up to the fact that the church today is not necessarily dying, but rather changing and needs to change. Pioneering fresh expressions of church that are courageous in their witness, creative in their community life, and less institutional is essential. Nevertheless, unless an ongoing, intentional effort invests in and equips pioneers, our efforts may eventually fade away, and those of us who are involved may suffer from exhaustion and burnout. The needs in the community are endless, so our self-care and the support of others are both critical. We are grateful to the Anabaptist Mennonite Network for the support offered through the Incarnate initiative.

We are excited to be part of this journey!

9

PEACEFUL BORDERS

Juliet Kilpin

BEGINNINGS

Peaceful Borders, a project of the Anabaptist Mennonite Network, works to support asylum seekers, refugees, and migrants to build communities of mutual support and solidarity that help new arrivals forge successful lives in a new country. We do this by initiating refugee-led community hubs alongside bespoke one-to-one support to accompany people as they navigate their new life. We currently work primarily with asylum seekers and refugees who are in long-term hotel and hostel accommodation and who struggle to access adequate information and assistance to do the things that will help them build a new life in the UK. We look for what God is doing on the margins and seek to join in.

My work now is informed by my previous experience with Urban Expression, which I cofounded in 1997 and helped to flesh out the founding values of this urban church planting movement. (Many of these are explored in my book *Urban to the Core.*[1]) These values—of relationship, humility, and creativity—are frequently described as Anabaptist in nature.

They have flowed through my veins and my priorities since that time, as has a deep interest in urbanization and how we are responding to it. In fact, one of the agitations that birthed Urban Expression was a frustration that so few of the 1990s church planting exploits were focusing on urban communities, where the majority of people live.

Peaceful Borders emerged in the summer of 2015, when British prime minister David Cameron declared that, on the edge of the port city of Calais in northern France, a "swarm of migrants" was trying to get to the UK.[2] The impression the public was given was that returning vacationers were being attacked and harassed as a multitude of people attempted to find a way to cross the English Channel to claim asylum. People I knew canceled their summer holidays out of fear of being attacked in Calais.

The number of people fleeing conflict and oppression on the borders of Europe was indeed growing exponentially in 2015. The war raging in Syria was creating a new movement of people that only added to those fleeing other conflicts in Afghanistan, Ethiopia, Eritrea, Sudan, Iran, and beyond.

Calais has always been a "departure city" for those seeking sanctuary in the UK, but in August 2015 this so-called "refugee crisis" saw a small informal settlement of a few hundred people in a forest grow to one thousand. The authorities were becoming concerned. This "jungle," as those encamped there termed it, could no longer be hidden in the trees.

When these troubled human beings were called a "swarm" by the most powerful man in the UK, something inside me snapped. As a coordinator and church planter with Urban Expression, I frequently encountered deep suspicion and dislike of urban communities. It was difficult to recruit ministers to inner-city churches—the suburbs seemed much more attractive. We often had to challenge myths that the London borough of Tower Hamlets was violent, unfriendly, and scary. Here, in "arrival cities" like London, generations of migrants throughout history have placed their feet on the first rung of a ladder. But people from the largely monocultural suburbs were apprehensive about these multicultural urban communities. I recognized the same demonizing myths now being peddled about refugees in Calais.

I connected on social media with others who expressed similar concerns, and a small group of us decided to visit Calais in search of the truth. We reached out to a charity in Calais and offered to bring useful items in exchange for a learning visit. We met one August morning at the Maidstone service station and traveled in a convoy of cars via the Eurotunnel. In France, thirty-five minutes later, we drove to a church that L'Auberge Des Migrants, a humanitarian organization, was using as a warehouse. We emptied our cars of what we had hoped might be useful items, but we struggled to find space to put them in the warehouse. It had the air of a charity shop that had simply become overwhelmed with too many donations and too few volunteers.

After this, the charity coordinator took us to the informal camp, where approximately one thousand refugees and asylum seekers from all corners of the world were now living among the shrubs. We were nervous—we didn't know what to expect—but we were determined to listen to local wisdom rather than British media scaremongering. That afternoon exposed me to experiences that caused a profound paradigm shift for me. It held up a mirror to the realities of an urbanized world, where those who simply want to build a life are forbidden to set up a tent, those who seek safety are teargassed by the police, those who desire safe travel have no legal routes, those who seek agency are considered stateless, those who crave dignity are othered, those who say they are all but dead already have no choice but to risk everything for a good chance at life.

After an astonishing afternoon of assisting volunteers with food distributions, talking and drinking tea with residents— who insisted they serve us and share their stories—and avoiding the overflowing portable toilets, we jumped in our cars, refused the polite requests to transport individuals to the UK, and headed home. As we traveled safely and effortlessly on the Eurotunnel to Folkestone, we stood to reflect but were unable to find words to express what we had seen. The scale, the friendliness, the hospitality, the sadness, the desperation, the injustice. All on our doorstep.

Such a paradigm shift compelled me to return to help, to understand, to witness. When people asked what it was like in Calais, I could not find the words to explain. "You just have to come and see it for yourself," I would reply. My long-term friend and collaborator Simon Jones, who was on the steering group for the London Urban Expression teams, was one of the first to come with me and was equally transfixed. Bromley Baptist Church, where he was a minister, allowed him to use some time to visit regularly, and Spurgeon's College, where he lectured, encouraged him to take students to learn, witness, and reflect. Urban Expression trustees allowed me to use some of my time to visit Calais, and a serendipitously timed donation from Tonbridge Baptist Church enabled me to give up some work that was significantly less inspiring, which gave me more time still. We formed a team and were soon visiting Calais one day each week.

While we were not completely sure about our distinct role, our imbued Anabaptist values shaped our approach. We wanted to listen and learn through building relationships, and we wanted to bear witness to the atrocities and resilience we encountered. We wanted to learn how to be good news to the powerless and persecuted in this place and to learn from the simple living and generous sharing that was evident. We wanted to follow the peaceful way of Jesus and understand how we could work for justice. In this camp, which was currently peaceful but had all the contributing compounds of division and violence, we felt compelled to promote nonviolence and explore how to sustain peace between diverse individuals and nationalities in this liminal space.

To begin with, we assisted however we could. We brought things—tents and sleeping bags, medical supplies, jackets, and infant formula. We even arranged to transport donated caravans, or trailers, to protect the most vulnerable during the winter. The camp was growing rapidly, almost one thousand new people each month. Every week I visited, it changed. New tents, new distribution points, new streets, even new shops. A shantytown was growing before our eyes. As the camp grew, so did the number of mostly British volunteers who were coming over. Many came, like we did, for a short visit. But many were so horrified and transfixed that they could not return home. Inexperienced humanitarians who wanted to share mutual aid raised money, rented warehouses, and distributed things in a more orderly manner. Volunteers from within and beyond the camp set up rudimentary family centers, libraries, schools, kitchens, churches, and mosques. A city built of wooden pallets was rising.

Two groups of people stood out to us at this point. The first was young volunteers who were swamped with responsibility, anger, and exhaustion as they attempted to fix the situation. The second was a spontaneous, organic emergence of refugee community leaders from every nationality present whose community members were looking to them for advice, safety, and sustenance. We also noticed that while delivery of vital supplies was being coordinated more and more efficiently, it was not without its tensions, because each group had its own preferred ways of doing things.

Peacemaking had an important role to play. In a volatile, unpredictable environment, we prepared ourselves for conflict resolution, took time to pastor the burnt-out volunteers, and asked the community leaders what they needed to be heard more clearly. These things became our focus. We did not need a name for our project and resisted this for some time (even though so many new projects were being born). But when the French CRS security police[3] and other police officers started to demand ID at the entrances to the camp, we decided that it might help if we, too, had a lanyard to show. Within a week or two we had a name, a logo, and lanyards—and Peaceful Borders was born.

EYES OPEN

Having witnessed the realities of the camp over numerous visits, I felt an imperative to tell the truth about the situation. The narrative of the media and politicians was so inexorably negative toward migrants in Calais that those of us who were getting to know them as individuals wanted to defend them and their right to safety. Many of us privileged volunteers had never witnessed state violence before, but now we were witnessing refugees being dropped off at the camp shoeless by police who had caught them trying to cross the Channel and decided to punish them by removing their only pair of shoes. "Shoes? Shoes? Shoes?" will always echo in my mind as a memory of desperate requests.

One evening, as I sat in a café made of pallets and tarps, I heard pops and then shouts from people as tear gas canisters landed in the camp. CRS officers fired them from the adjoining motorway into the camp for no apparent reason other than to intimidate. They fell among teenagers, babies, and adults alike. It was here that I learned the value of always wearing a scarf and having Tiger Balm to wipe under your nose. The number of tear gas canisters lying around the camp was shocking. Tear gas does nothing but make people scared and angry. In resistance, some made works of art out of the canisters and displayed them prominently.

Once when I was leaving, I walked past a group of men carrying an unconscious man to the outskirts of the camp. The man was having a seizure. They had called emergency services, but the ambulance would not enter the camp, so they carried the man to the road. I waited with them in solidarity and concern, witnessing, praying. We stood beside the road and watched the ambulance drive by, refusing to stop. Fire engines would not enter the camp either. Yet incidents caused by open fires and candles were frequent. Residents and volunteers organized their own fire trucks, which were stored in the camp, ready to respond.

At the end of another day, my colleague and I walked up what had become the high street of the camp. Ahead of us was a larger than usual group of refugees, maybe twenty people. They were agitated, but not at us, so although apprehensive, we continued to walk confidently through the group. As we emerged, ahead of us were four CRS officers pointing rifles directly at the men. Now finding the guns aiming directly at us, we must have subconsciously decided, in our white Western privilege, to continue walking. The officers lowered their weapons and shuffled aside. The group of refugees disbanded.

Only some meters behind the CRS did we stop and process what had just happened. Why these men deserved such aggression was a mystery. But we were aware that our privilege could be used to diffuse tension and prevent harm.

Although in France, the camp was like a mirror held up to the UK. It reflected our policies and processes and the funds the Home Office paid France to keep people out. I felt complicit in the injury being caused to people. "If you can't help us, don't harm us," one wise community leader said. But the UK was heaping harm upon harm, and as voting residents, we were complicit in our ignorance and inaction.

SOLIDARITY AND MUTUAL AID

Getting involved in mutual aid was one way to alleviate the sense of complicity. Volunteers chose instead to stand in solidarity with the residents of the camp and to share what they could. Many gave up stability, jobs, homes, and partners in order to help those in need. We felt we were witnessing a moment in history and wanted to be able to respond positively when asked in the future, "What did you do?" Groups crammed into apartments and trailers in order to save on the costs of living in Calais while serving in this way. It was not dissimilar to when our Urban Expression team moved into Shadwell in East London and we shared accommodations, meals, and costs to enable us all to serve a community to which we felt called.

And residents in the camp did likewise, if not more so. With so many coming from cultures that are more communally minded than in the West, there was much more "we" than "me" present among the refugee community. We witnessed exuberant gestures of generosity and kindness as people gave their only shoes to those going crazy with despair, invited new arrivals to share their tiny tent until the next distribution, and shared food, warmth, and essentials of survival. That is what they were all seeking to do—survive.

Volunteers were quickly getting burnt out. Each week we could see them becoming more exhausted and frenetic. The most burnt out would talk incessantly and looked haggard and traumatized. Our Peaceful Borders team decided that one thing we could do was resist the urge to race around and instead take time to listen to the volunteers we met. We were considerably older than many, so we could offer a shoulder to lean on and possibly a word of comfort or advice. Or a word of permission to go home and rest. Some experienced humanitarian psychotherapists offered their assistance in this regard. We helped them set up the Solidarity and Support Network, which provided opportunities for volunteers, including us, to check in regularly on the phone with someone with professional expertise. More recently, we have helped some former volunteers receive professional counseling as they continue to process what they experienced.

ACCOMPANYING

As we worked to support the volunteers, we soon noticed refugee community leaders who were evidently looking beyond their own needs and survival in the camp and organizing for the welfare of their peers. We were introduced to Samer from Sudan, who took us to meet others from his community. They had organized themselves with communal spaces, which provided warmth and space to cook, and there was always a warm welcome and sweet spiced tea.

The Ethiopian community leaders had built a church out of pallets and adorned it with pictures and tissue paper. It was rudimentary but sacred for anyone who wanted to pray.

An eternal barrel of fire at the entrance to the church provided a warm welcome and a frequent feast of beans. The
singing and the drumming in the services brought me to
tears. It became a pilgrimage for me to start each day with a
moment of quiet prayer in this church. It was grounding for
my spirituality and my deeds. The words of the Lord's Prayer
have never made more sense to me than while praying it in this
church while bulldozers crunched and ripped down half the
camp on the other side of the tarps. "Forgive our trespasses as
we forgive those who trespass against us. . . . Your will be done
on earth as in heaven."

The many cafés that opened provided themed community spaces. They felt simultaneously like the most fake but
most real spaces in the whole of Calais. Was I in Afghanistan,
Eritrea, or Kurdistan? During the day, they charged volunteers
for chai, but at night, when most volunteers were gone, they
fed the residents of the camp for free, letting new arrivals sleep
there until tents could be provided the next day.

I began to hear about the fledgling work of Safe Passage,
a project emerging from Citizens UK, which was deeply concerned about the hundreds of unaccompanied children in the
camp and bemused by how the French and British governments seemed oblivious to their safety or fate. Having visited
the camp regularly, I offered to help Safe Passage founder
George Gabriel in this vital work in any way possible. He
asked if I could visit the Syrian community leader who had
offered to make a list of all the Syrian children who were trying to reach family in the UK. I did, and we visited, drinking
coffee as he showed me the growing list. I reassured him that
the Safe Passage team members were doing all they could to
mobilize a legal team to take the Home Office to court for
not implementing its responsibilities. As a member of the

European Union at that time, the UK was obliged to enact the Dublin III Regulation, which legislates that children in one EU country have the right to seek reunion with family members in another EU country. But the Home Office was not processing such claims.

All of these community leaders had things in common. They were looking out for the welfare of others before themselves and had an innate understanding of what their communities—and the camp as a whole—needed in order to prevent more harm being done to them. One afternoon, Simon and I visited the Kabul Café in the camp, and after paying for our chai, we noticed a couple of key volunteers sitting with some of these community leaders we had met. We were invited to sit at the table with them. We listened as they discussed concerns about food distributions and proposed more humane ways of giving out food so that the Sudanese could cook for themselves in their community kitchens. They shared concerns about disparate volunteers giving out tents and sleeping bags, because they couldn't know whether people were taking more than they needed and preventing those in need from getting supplies. They proposed their own community-based distribution centers in the camp, where community leaders could oversee things. They shared concerns about lack of toilets and water, which might lead to disease, and these issues were taken to the sanitary company tasked with oversight of the informal camp.

Simon and I sat in silence. We didn't feel it was our place to comment. But at the end, the community leaders asked us for our thoughts. We simply reflected back what we had heard them say. We were invited to join them each week from then on and had the privilege of accompanying them in their vital task of protecting the community as it grew from three thousand to ten thousand. I remember one particularly special walk with them as they prepared for the demolition of half the camp by the authorities and accurately predicted that residents would simply relocate to the other side. They walked and discussed, then climbed a mound of sand to look over the tents and canopies of the camp and pointed out the places where new tents could go when the time came. It had more than a slight resonance with watching Moses looking over the promised land and giving instructions.

While the community leaders generously looked out for others, it was not without its cost. They were on their own journey to safety and had their own families to reunite with. Some delayed their own transit to assist in this important work. They encouraged unaccompanied children to trust the work of Safe Passage and wait for legal reunion rather than risk their lives using irregular travel. We felt a pull to accompany these remarkable leaders and support them in such vital work.

CONFLICT RESOLUTION

There were also times when the newly forming charities that were growing out of their mutual commitments to help clashed in their priorities and practices. They didn't always listen well to community leaders. In building relationship with all the volunteers, we were sometimes able to hold space for the conflict and help bring resolution.

When parts of the camp were demolished, we stood alongside residents to ensure that they were given time to remove their few belongings. Once, an area of caravan trailers was surrounded by CRS officers prior to demolition. We kept watch as peacemakers. Earlier in the day, children had been told by the French authorities to walk a mile to a warehouse for processing for travel to the UK. After walking to the warehouse only to discover nothing was happening there, one young Sudanese boy tried to return to his caravan but was not allowed in. Everything he owned was in the caravan, including his documents. We spoke calmly in rudimentary French to the CRS officer, who ignored us. We continued to repeat the concern that the boy's documents were in the caravan and he needed to get them before it was demolished. We continued to be ignored. We kept our calm and asked for his supervisor. Eventually, a more senior officer came and finally allowed the boy access if we accompanied him. I remember standing with him as he took his small suitcase and rushed to pack anything he could find. He was scared. I urged him to slow down and to think. He had time. Nothing would happen while we were with him. The image of him sitting on his suitcase watching his caravan with bemusement about what might be next will stay with me forever. He was a child. The authorities had just taken away his one place of safety and had not provided an alternative.

For a month, a group of Christian Iranian men went on hunger strike because they were so furious about their inhumane treatment. Not only did they stop eating, but they sewed their lips together in protest. We watched them do this, as did a horde of journalists. As the men grew weaker, community leaders were asked to visit them and implore them to stop. I walked with one Muslim community leader, who asked what might be a good thing to say from a Christian perspective. Hunger striking was a new pastoral issue for me, but we explored some common scriptural themes and stories. On another occasion, I visited and was able to pray for the men. I also took senior faith leaders from the UK to visit them so that they could understand and help amplify their voices.

After a significant fight in the camp, which resulted in a fire and some destruction, my colleague Simon arrived to find the Sudanese and Afghan community leaders calling their community members to a meeting. In this large tent, the two community leaders spoke and apologized for their lack of leadership. They felt that if they had been better leaders, their communities would not have fought. They were not dishing out individual judgment but modeling communal responsibility. They preached about brotherhood and unity and made each Afghan shake the hand of each Sudanese. After this, the Afghan imam prayed a spontaneous, exuberant prayer, and the Spirit of God was tangible.

ONGOING CAMPAIGNING AND SOLIDARITY
Most people who lived in the camp for any amount of time, or volunteered there, have remained deeply and personally connected in the world of migration. Either they and their families are themselves displaced, or a substantial number of friends are. They have solidarity with the story of twenty-first-century migration. Therefore, every headline about a shipwreck, or a rescue boat in the Mediterranean that is not being allowed to dock, or a small boat that has made it to Kent, or the latest scheme to create deterrents, resonates intensely. The pull to remain engaged in the issues and offer caring responses is strong because the injustices remain profound and dehumanizing. With the inevitability of urbanization and climate change, they also remain undiminished.

Providing temporary respite for the most vulnerable in a safe house was one way we helped in 2016. We remain deeply committed to the community of volunteers who built this ministry and who continue to create safe space in Calais for the hundreds who continue to pass through the city in search of sanctuary.

Campaigning for change is another way we channeled our anger at injustice. I could not believe the number of unaccompanied children I saw in the Calais camp in 2015 and 2016. One tangible contribution I could make was to support the Safe Passage team that was working to open safe routes. We met many children who had family in the UK. The community leaders were foundational in building relationships with them and gently coaxing from them the necessary information that could strengthen their case for reunion. UK-based team members contacted family members to confirm the connections and explore any issues that might build the case. I remember using simple multilingual videos that explained who might be eligible for a Dublin III reunion and playing them to children I met. If children fit the criteria, I asked a community leader to talk with them.

We used community organizing methodology to increase the power to bring about change. We brought religious leaders from the UK over to witness and then return home to enthuse their denominations to take action and support the campaign. Social workers came over in their spare time to do the required best-interest interviews with the children, and volunteer interpreters helped with translation. Lawyers in the UK took the case of three children and one vulnerable adult to the Royal Courts of Justice. One rainy evening in January 2016, I received a phone call saying we had won the case. It was a landmark legal ruling that opened up one legal route for family reunion. I shouted in joy and disbelief. I pondered this alien feeling of victory. It felt triumphant. The following day the four young people were on the Eurostar to London. A crowd of supporters waited outside St. Pancras station to welcome the first of many children to find safety.

A second route to safety was opened up by Lord Alf Dubs, with whom Safe Passage worked to propose an amendment to the Immigration Bill in 2016. This "Dubs Amendment"[4] made it possible for an agreed number of unaccompanied children to come to the UK. I organized faith leaders to write to members of Parliament in support of this amendment, and together we learned how to make systemic change.

In October 2016, the French authorities decisively demolished the camp. I remember crisp autumn mornings in Calais, running around after individuals who had been successfully selected for this expedited process of safe travel to the UK, to ensure they made it onto the waiting buses. Between February and October 2016, 900 unaccompanied children came to the UK, including 250 through the Dubs Scheme. To date, Safe Passage has helped 1,800 children reach safety.

Immediately after the demolition of the Calais camp, the work of Peaceful Borders centered around many of these children who had been successfully transferred via these efforts. In the following years, we also supported key community leaders who had arrived in the UK as they organized mutual aid and care for diaspora communities. Hopetowns, conceived by Samer, provided a weekly space in northwest London where people could come for coffee, English classes, and help with filling out forms, opening bank accounts, and getting accommodation when the Home Office gave them twenty-eight days to leave their temporary accommodation after they were given leave to remain. When funding allowed, our priority was to build our Peaceful Borders team with these community leaders who had invaluable lived-experience of journeying to and settling in the UK.

When the Home Office sent people to a disused army facility, Napier Barracks, in 2019, we worked with other local volunteers to help open a weekly drop-in center at a nearby church. Here we offered social and therapeutic activities, food, and when possible, access to legal assistance. We worked closely with the Humans for Rights Network to bear witness to the situation and monitor systemic concerns that arose. We met unaccompanied minors whom the Home Office had placed in the adult barracks and engaged lawyers to get them moved to safety as quickly as possible. We bought these children phones so lawyers could actually contact them. We met men whose mental or physical health needs were not being met, and we sought to give assistance and challenge the management to provide access to doctors. We supported those bringing legal challenges to their unjust situations.

In 2020, we heard that the Home Office was putting unaccompanied children into children's hotels. This was deeply concerning, and we managed to visit one and connected with those who were given more access than we were to gauge the problematic issues. Humans for Rights Network received phone calls from children in these hotels, who expressed concerns about lack of care and often a desire to be free to go and live with family already in the UK.

At the outbreak of COVID-19, the Home Office contracted with many hotels to accommodate asylum seekers. On the one hand, this ensured some shelter during the early stages of the pandemic, but we became very concerned about the conditions in these hotels, especially hostels that were accommodating people in dormitories, which provided no space for social distancing and meager sanitary conditions. One such hostel, in King's Cross, came to our attention. With the Folkestone support group running well without us, we decided to replicate the model and approached King's Cross Baptist Church about using their hall to run a similar drop-in center. Men from Sudan, Syria, Ethiopia, Eritrea, Iran, Iraq, and beyond attended. Their stories were so familiar.

After the British government airlifted people from Kabul, Afghanistan, and the war broke out in Ukraine, we met numerous Afghans and a Ukrainian who had fallen through the gaps in their resettlement schemes or arrived via other means. Those not from these chosen countries sensed the inconsistencies in their treatment. We even met a few Russians, some of the millions of young men who didn't want to fight but introduced themselves with a whisper for fear of being vilified for their nation's crimes.

All of those who arrive in the UK need help navigating an increasingly hostile environment, where even the ironically named Home Office–sponsored charity Migrant Help struggles to help. Refugees frequently lack access to healthcare, legal assistance, decent food, and basic dignity. Post-Brexit UK has yet to agree to bilateral agreements replacing Dublin III, meaning that fewer reunions are currently possible. Home Office backlogs mean that hotel accommodation is becoming normalized, and the threat of removal to Rwanda leaves those seeking sanctuary fearful of further involuntary displacement. At the time of writing, the UK government's new Illegal Immigration Bill is being implemented. It embeds in law the removal of new arrivals to a safe third country and denies them the opportunity to make an asylum claim. A recent Home Office policy change has also reduced the twenty-eight-day notice to leave accommodations to seven days, resulting in rapidly increasing homelessness of those who have been granted asylum.

GOD IN THE "JUNGLE"

Anabaptist convictions, which animate the work of Peaceful Borders, center the life of Jesus in theology. The New

Testament depicts a dispossessed Middle Eastern person facing oppression and migration. His parables highlighted systemic injustice and challenged individual selfishness and greed. He taught what was necessary for a fulfilled life. His transient life relied on hospitality, given and received. He was a leader in his community and beyond, with many who followed his wisdom. Jesus knew his identity but was quick to serve and sacrifice his life for others.

When we first visited Calais, we were asking ourselves where God was and what God was doing. It was not difficult to see God in the people who shared many of Jesus' characteristics. Some atheist volunteers even found God in the "jungle" because of what they saw in the lives of those who found themselves there.

Anabaptist values help us to be open to meeting God in others. Focusing on relationship, mutuality, simplicity, and humility enables us to follow the peaceful way. There will always be boundaries at the ends of nations and at the edges of our own lives. In these liminal, abrasive spaces, peaceful borders are possible and essential.

CONCLUSION

The Anabaptist Vision in Post-Christendom

The Anabaptist Mennonite Network in the UK is one of several neo-Anabaptist networks in societies with little or no historical Anabaptist or Mennonite presence. We have enjoyed forging connections with networks in Australia and New Zealand, Scandinavia, South Africa, and Korea, and we have links with projects and communities in several other nations. Some of the networks have adopted or slightly adapted our core convictions, and neo-Anabaptists in various nations have drawn on and facilitated translations of *The Naked Anabaptist.*

In most cases, these networks were galvanized by the ministries of North American Mennonite mission workers, some of whom spent decades in these contexts.[1] Their experience, resources, witness, and friendships were foundational to what has emerged, and the networks continue to learn from communities in Europe and North America that trace their origins to the sixteenth-century Anabaptists. But these networks are now mostly led by neo-Anabaptist followers of Jesus, who are

exploring ways of contextualizing and incarnating the Anabaptist vision in their societies.

The practices that we have explored in this book are those
which neo-Anabaptists in the UK believe will help shape missional communities and initiatives in our context—practices that
resonate with the historical Anabaptist tradition but are being
reimagined for our twenty-first-century post-Christendom society. We suspect that neo-Anabaptists in other post-Christendom
societies will likely endorse many of these practices, but some
may have greater priority than others in different nations, and
there may well be further practices that other networks identify as significant in their contexts. Neo-Anabaptists in South
Africa, for example, are exploring the interaction between
Anabaptism and African theologies, and reflecting on the relevance of the Anabaptist vision in a post-apartheid society. And
in other nations that are not emerging from the Christendom
era, the priorities and practices of neo-Anabaptists might be
quite different. Earlier chapters have drawn on postcolonial
as well as post-Christendom perspectives and have acknowledged differences in other cultural contexts, but the primary
focus has been on the expression and implementation of these
practices within a particular context.

These, then, are some of the limitations of this book. The
practices are those that we believe are contextually significant
in post-Christendom societies and specifically in the UK. We
are aware of ongoing debates in America (but not in Can-
ada) about the pertinence of the notion of post-Christendom.
Many are convinced that America is following the trend of
European nations, albeit some decades later, and point to
growing evidence of this. This is certainly our perception
from across the Atlantic. Some argue that America cannot
be moving into post-Christendom, because the constitutional

separation of church and state precludes America from ever being described as a Christendom society. But this argument seems to ignore the capacity of the Christendom ideology to adapt to various social and political realities. Others continue to regard the United States as a Christian nation, conflate the kingdom of God with the American dream, and advocate strategies to restore the influence of Christianity in all areas of public life (in effect, retaining or restoring an American expression of Christendom). If, as we believe, post-Christendom is advancing in America, we hope that the practices and perspectives explored in this book might be helpful to those who are engaging with this emerging reality, perhaps even to Mennonites and other historical Anabaptists, offering some fresh angles on familiar practices.

PRACTICES AND SPIRITUALITY

This book has other limitations. Just as the core convictions examined in *The Naked Anabaptist* were presented not as a comprehensive account of what neo-Anabaptists believe, but as features of the Anabaptist vision that inspired and challenged us, so we do not presume that the common practices explored in earlier chapters represent a complete list of practices that might characterize neo-Anabaptist communities, even in our own context. Nor has this book grappled adequately with various challenges to and criticisms of these practices. These include a concern that identifying an interpretive center of Scripture risks imposing meanings on other texts; important questions about safeguarding and power dynamics in relation to the practice of mutual accountability; and the limited scope of the examples offered of peace witness. Readers will likely have identified other inadequacies. But we hope that this book will stimulate further discussion that can help us nuance and extend the application of these practices and identify other important ones. And, of course, we gratefully recognize that practices rooted in other Christian traditions are also important for Anabaptist communities to thrive in post-Christendom societies.

After all, as Canadian Mennonite Tom Yoder Neufeld warned me, listing only those practices that are distinctively Anabaptist does not do justice to the concern of the early Anabaptists to discover and recover practices that characterized the churches in the New Testament. He counseled us, as the Anabaptist Mennonite Network was trying to identify distinctive common practices, to construct "a full-orbed list rather than only distinctives, which then sometimes take over as the whole list."[2] Attempting to cover a full-orbed range of practices in this book would have made it unwieldy, but it is important to include this caveat and to heed the warning that distinctive practices are not thereby more important than practices shared with other Christian traditions. The practices we have explored are, we believe, distinctively though not uniquely Anabaptist, but there are many other practices that neo-Anabaptist communities will value because they are historical and contemporary Christian practices.

Furthermore, we have only recently embarked on the initiative to plant Anabaptist churches, and the projects described by my colleagues are only a few years old, so we are still testing out the practices which we believe are distinctive and missionally potent. That is the significance of the term *emerging* in the subtitle of this book. What we have offered here is tentative and exploratory. But we believe it may be helpful to explore these practices now in order to spark the imagination of those who are pioneering new communities and offer them resources for this task.

Much more could also be written about the personal and communal spirituality that undergirds the practices we have examined. I have attempted to follow through on the commitment in the early pages of this book to make explicit links between the common practices and the role of the Holy Spirit. The Anabaptist tradition certainly emphasizes discipleship and ethical behavior, but the early Anabaptists knew that they needed the power of the Spirit to live faithfully in the face of great opposition. Although early Anabaptists sometimes used the language of justification, other terminology is prominent in their writings: new birth, illumination, enlightenment, the new creature, and regeneration. Their understanding of grace was that it not only dealt with past sins but enabled forgiven sinners to live differently. Righteousness was imparted as well as imputed. The grace of God was efficacious, transforming human nature. As Leonhard Schiemer, an early Austrian Anabaptist, declared: "Those who do not feel in themselves a power about which they have to say that things that were once impossible are now possible are not yet born again of water and spirit, even the Holy Spirit."[3]

Anabaptists also expected the Spirit to be at work in their gatherings, prompting one after another to contribute, giving insight into the Scriptures, inspiring them to sing, stirring them to pray, enabling them to exercise their spiritual gifts, and uniting them together. Some were more exuberant, others more sober, but all recognized their need of God's grace if they were to follow Jesus, build communities, stand firm in the face of suffering, and bear witness to their neighbors.

Neo-Anabaptist communities will be no less in need of the Spirit's empowering and guidance on the margins of post-Christendom. There are, of course, rich resources in many other traditions, although some of these might be reimagined and reworked in line with particular Anabaptist convictions and priorities. An example of this is the Anabaptist prayer book *Take Our Moments and Our Days*, which adapts a familiar pattern of morning and evening prayer and imbues it with Anabaptist perspectives.[4] Many of us have used this resource personally, in our families, in our study groups, and at conferences. We are grateful for several collections of prayers and reflections from the sixteenth century and subsequent generations that are infused with Anabaptist spirituality.[5] And our communities will no doubt also want to explore ways of contextualizing two distinctive aspects of Anabaptist spirituality: following (*Nachfolge*) and yieldedness (*Gelassenheit*).

HABITS

When I was searching for a suitable title for this book, one which connected in some way with the imagery of *The Naked Anabaptist*, a member of our Anabaptist group in East Kent suggested "Anabaptist Habits." I was attracted by this idea, which was a creative way of combining a form of monastic clothing for "naked Anabaptists" with the notion of regular practices and spiritual formation.[6]

As I considered this, I recalled a conference the Anabaptist Network cosponsored with the Northumbria Community several years ago when we explored Celtic, Anabaptist, and new monastic spirituality. We called this "New Habits for a New Era." Presenting a paper on Anabaptism at that event, I mentioned that the Anabaptists were sometimes accused by their sixteenth-century opponents of being monkish. Martin Luther accused them of having a "monkish" life and doctrine.[7] Ulrich Zwingli claimed they were "restoring a full monkish system."[8] And the Strasbourg reformer Wolfgang Capito detected "the beginning of a new monasticism."[9] There have been several suggestions over the past few decades that our post-Christendom context requires a new kind of monasticism. The earliest and most frequently quoted is a statement from a letter written by Dietrich Bonhoeffer: "The restoration of the church will surely come only from a new type of monasticism which has nothing in common with the old but a complete lack of compromise in a life lived in accordance with the Sermon on the Mount in the discipleship of Christ. I think it is time to gather people together to do this."[10] More recently, Andrew Walker wrote: "We will have to return to structures . . . akin to the monastery, the religious community and the sect . . . we will need to create sectarian plausibility structures in order for our story to take hold of our congregations and root them in the gospel."[11]

I also remembered that the title of one of the chapters in David Augsburger's *Dissident Discipleship* addresses "habitual humility," and that several of the other chapter titles imply habitual behavior: "stubborn loyalty," "tenacious serenity," and "resolute nonviolence." And in *Practices: Mennonite Worship and Witness*, John D. Roth explores the connection between practices and habits as he reflects on the role of the community in character formation. He defines character as "engrained habits, dispositions, and assumptions, formed over time in the context of a community, that express our deepest understanding of how the world works."[12]

I also looked again at the book I coedited with James Krabill in 2011 to celebrate the legacy of Alan and Eleanor Kreider, entitled *Forming Christian Habits in Post-Christendom*. We acknowledged that there was "no attempt in this volume to set forth a list of *all* the Christian habits that will be necessary for the church living in a post-Christendom era."[13] But we were drawn to the notion of habits as we thought about communities in post-Christendom and practices that needed to be embedded. We also referred to a book edited by Dorothy Bass and Craig Dykstra, *Practicing Our Faith: A Way of Life for a Searching People*, which contains a list of twelve practices, some of which overlap with the common practices we have explored. Bass and Dykstra describe the practice of Christian habits as "rehearsing a way of life."[14]

But though I was strongly tempted by the idea of calling the book "Anabaptist Habits," I concluded that this was precipitate. Neo-Anabaptist communities and initiatives in the UK are not yet well enough established to have developed engrained habits or to have rehearsed them as a way of life. I hope that the practices we have explored in this book might become habits, instincts, and reflexes, but time will tell. We will need to find ways, as more Anabaptist communities and initiatives emerge, to reflect on and share together our experiences, honing, critiquing, and developing our practices.

The Naked Anabaptist retold the story of Dirk Willems, perhaps the best known of all Anabaptist stories. It is a poignant and challenging story of enemy-loving by a young sixteenth-century follower of Jesus.[15] It also poses questions about the ethos and practices of the Anabaptist community to which Willems belonged in Asperen. How had they nurtured this young man so that he responded as he did in a situation where he had no time to consider his options but acted reflexively? What communal practices had shaped his character and prompted him to this instinctive act of courageous and selfless love? Perhaps in time the common practices we have identified and begun to embody might become habits and give us the courage as neo-Anabaptists to live as faithfully, counterintuitively, and reflexively as Willems and many of the other early Anabaptists.

Post-Christendom is a challenging environment. But it is also a context with plenty of opportunities for pioneering creative mission initiatives, planting new churches, reimagining the relationship between gospel and culture, retelling the biblical story, and learning to live as followers of Jesus on the margins of society. We will need the insights and resources of many Christian traditions if we are to respond faithfully to these challenges and opportunities, but we dare to hope that the Anabaptist tradition can make a distinctive contribution.

CORE CONVICTIONS

From the Anabaptist Mennonite Network

1. Jesus is our example, teacher, friend, redeemer, and Lord. He is the source of our life, the central reference point for our faith and lifestyle, for our understanding of church and our engagement with society. We are committed to following Jesus as well as worshiping him.

2. Jesus is the focal point of God's revelation. We are committed to a Jesus-centered approach to the Bible, and to the community of faith as the primary context in which we read the Bible and discern and apply its implications for discipleship.

3. Western culture is slowly emerging from the Christendom era, when church and state jointly presided over a society in which almost all were assumed to be Christian. Whatever its positive contributions on values and institutions, Christendom seriously distorted the gospel, marginalized Jesus, and has left the churches ill-equipped for mission in a post-Christendom culture. As we reflect on this, we are committed to learning from the experience and perspectives of movements such as

Anabaptism that rejected standard Christendom assumptions and pursued alternative ways of thinking and behaving.

4. The frequent association of the church with status, wealth, and force is inappropriate for followers of Jesus and damages our witness. We are committed to vulnerability and to exploring ways of being good news to the poor, powerless, and persecuted, aware that such discipleship may attract opposition, resulting in suffering and sometimes ultimately martyrdom.

5. Churches are called to be committed communities of discipleship and mission, places of friendship, mutual accountability, and multivoiced worship. As we eat together, sharing bread and wine, we sustain hope as we seek God's kingdom together. We are committed to nurturing and developing such churches, in which young and old are valued, leadership is consultative, roles are related to gifts rather than gender, and baptism is for believers.

6. Spirituality and economics are inter-connected. In an individualist and consumerist culture and in a world where economic injustice is rife, we are committed to finding ways of living simply, sharing generously, caring for creation, and working for justice.

7. Peace is at the heart of the gospel. As followers of Jesus in a divided and violent world, we are committed to finding nonviolent alternatives and to learning how to make peace between individuals, within and among churches, in society, and between nations.

Appendix 2

COMMON PRACTICES

From the Anabaptist Mennonite Network

1. Interpreting and following the way of Jesus
2. Living simply
3. Multivoiced worship and biblical interpretation
4. Baptizing would-be disciples
5. Communion as a peace meal
6. Nonhierarchical leadership
7. Consensual decision-making
8. Practicing mutual accountability
9. Practicing peacemaking
10. Practicing mutual aid
11. Telling the truth
12. Witness in word and lifestyle

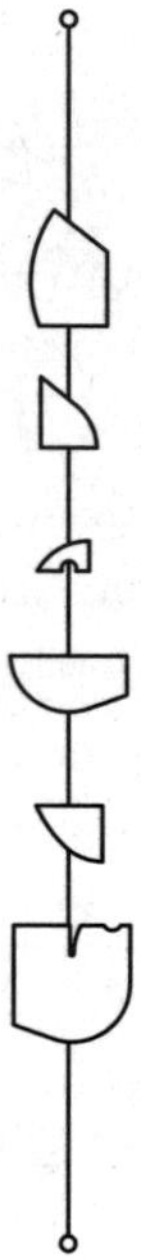

Appendix 3

GATHERING AROUND THE TABLE

An Anabaptist Table Liturgy

Words in *italic type* are signposts; the text need not be read aloud. Words in ***bold italic type*** are all said together. All other sentences can be led by anyone present.

THE WELCOME
Come, everything is ready. Happy are those who share in a meal in the kingdom of God.

A Song of the Kingdom

FINDING OUR PLACE
Jesus said, "Listen! I am standing at the door, knocking; if you hear my voice and open the door, I will come in to you and eat with you, and you with me."

We give thanks for this promise and for God's presence here with us.

God welcomes us and so we greet each other:

(Name), we welcome you to this table in the name of Christ, the bread of life.

Response: Amen, it's good to be here.

We remember those we carry in our hearts who are not at this table today.

We name people on our hearts today.

Whatever table they are at today, we pray that they will know the blessing of Christ who broke the bread.

Jesus said, "When you have supper, do not invite just your friends, or relatives, or those who are wealthy . . . but rather invite the poor and marginalized."

We confess to God the excuses we have made for not living in the kingdom of God.

For our distraction in this day

by neglecting God's offer of love and by ignoring the cries of the poor,

Lord have mercy.

For our diversion from your way

by speaking harsh words to our friends and by failing to love our enemies,

Lord have mercy.

For the evasion of our calling

to care for the earth which sustains us and to combat injustice which surrounds us,

Lord have mercy.

For our confusion of priorities

by seeking success and not faithfulness and by our failure to drench action with prayer, and embody prayer with action,

Lord, have mercy.

THE PROMISE OF NEW BEGINNINGS

The prophet Isaiah writes: On this mountain the Lord Almighty will prepare for all the peoples a feast of rich food, a banquet of well-aged wines—the best of meats and the finest of wines. God will destroy on this mountain the shroud that is cast over all peoples, the sheet that covers all nations: God will swallow up death forever. The Lord will wipe away the tears from all faces, and he will take away the disgrace of the people from all the earth, for the Lord has spoken. In that day they will say:

This is our God; we trusted in him and he saved us. This is the Lord for whom we have waited, let us rejoice and be glad.

Bread and wine are placed on the table.

While they were at the table, Jesus took a loaf of bread and, after giving thanks, he broke it and gave it to them, saying, "This is my body given for you. Each time you eat this, remember me." Then he took a cup of wine, and gave it to them saying, "This is my blood which is poured out for many. Each time you drink this, remember me."

Thank you, God, that ordinary things can become special when placed in your hands. Thank you that what is broken may be made whole and what is given is not wasted.

Bread is passed around, and when all are served . . .

Be gentle when you touch bread.

Let it not lie uncared for, unwanted.
There is so much beauty in bread,
*   beauty of sun and soil, beauty of patient toil.*
Winds and rain have caressed it;
Christ often blessed it.
Be gentle when you touch bread.[1]

We eat bread together.

Wine is poured, each serving another, and when all are served . . .

Be loving when you drink wine.

Let its color, life, and joy be celebrated.
There is so much beauty in wine,
*   beauty of self-giving, beauty of forgiving.*
Winds and rain have caressed it;

Christ often blessed it.
Be loving when you drink wine.

We drink wine together.

Let's say together . . .

Thank you, God, for love, for food, and for friends to share it with.

The first course is served, and we all eat together.

Let the conversation flow.

Food!

After the first course is finished, we say together these words, and go round the table as at the start of evening, naming each other.

Thank you, Lord, for this meal
     but we cannot live by bread alone.
We have shared it together
     because we need each other
     gathered around this table.
We need (name).

Response: And I need you.

Lord God, as we bring our prayers,
     we thank you that we can share
     in your kingdom of justice and peace.

We come in our poverty, not in our wealth,
  in our blindness, not with great faith,
  in our weakness, not in our strength.
You want your house to be full.
  so now we bring to you those who live
  in the wide and narrow streets of our world
  who need your love and light, your peace and healing.

Nightlights or candles may be lit as we name individuals or situations.

PRAYER FOR A NEW EARTH

God of all places and this place:
You promised a new earth where the hungry will feast
and the oppressed go free.

Come, Lord, build that place among us.

God of all times and this time:
You promised a new day when the fearful will laugh
and the sick find healing.

Come, Lord, speed that time among us.

God of all people, our God:
Take what we have and what we hope for
to make this a world where all people find good news.

We come, Lord, to share in the work of your kingdom,
until the new earth is created among us. Amen.

Dessert is served!

After dessert, we bring the meal to a close with one of these prayers, whichever is best for you.

A Sixteenth-Century Anabaptist Prayer
O God, preserve us in your keeping,
  that we may not faint and abandon your word.
Let us enjoy the faithfulness which you have shown
  through your Son, Jesus Christ.
Kindle in us the fire of divine love;
  lead us to practice love as your dear children.
Let the light of your divine glory illuminate us,
  that we may walk in it.
O God, we ask you for one thing more:
  send us your Holy Spirit,
  endue us with power,
  renew our hearts,
  and make us strong in you,
  that we may obey you
  and praise your name.
Amen.

An Evening Prayer
It is evening and night is drawing near. The night is for stillness.

Let us be still in the presence of God.

It is evening after a long day.

What has been done has been done.

What has not been done has not been done.

Let it be.

The night is dark.

Let our fears of the darkness of the world and of our lives rest in you.

The night is quiet.

Let the quietness of your peace enfold us, all dear to us, and all who have no peace.

A Song of Blessing
The night heralds the dawn.

Let us look expectantly to a new day, new joys, new possibilities.

Amen.

As needed, we are invited to help clear the table and wash the dishes, with thanks and joy.

STUDY GUIDE

SECTION I

1. How can we avoid the danger of downgrading other parts of Scripture if we insist on "starting with Jesus"?
2. Choose another biblical topic not explored in chapter 1 and investigate this by starting with the life and teaching of Jesus before turning to other scriptures.
3. How relevant are debates about infant baptism or believers baptism in post-Christendom contexts?
4. What aspects of the early Anabaptists' practices of baptism or communion do you find most challenging or inspirational?
5. Weighing the potential and dangers of multivoiced biblical interpretation and worship, are these practices worth pursuing?
6. How can consensual decision-making be integrated with inspirational and effective leadership?
7. Are there any circumstances where you think it would be right not to tell the truth?

8. How can mutual accountability be practiced without breaking confidentiality or abusing power?

9. How do you respond to the critique of tithing and charitable giving?

10. What does living simply mean in your context, and how can you assess this?

11. What can be done to rehabilitate evangelism in light of problems with its practices over many years?

12. What issues in your locality most require peacemaking initiatives, and how can you respond to these?

13. How might the "common practices" explored in this section be introduced or embedded in your church or community?

SECTION II

1. If you are interested in planting a new Anabaptist expression of faith community, to which of the core convictions and common practices are you most attracted? Which are the most challenging to you?

2. Any new Christian community can only be considered Anabaptist if it is engaging in active peacemaking and reconciliation work. To what extent do you agree?

3. Would you agree that there are those within your context who are deeply spiritual but feel they don't fit in church? If so, how might you seek ways to include them?

4. The Anabaptist Christocentric focus reminds us that Jesus took on our culture and our practices: what does it mean to be Jesus in your community/context?

5. What personal or practical borders are evident in your context, and how might Anabaptist values shape your response to them?

6. When have you received hospitality in ways that have surprised you? Reflect on what this is teaching you.

FOR FURTHER READING

ANABAPTISM IN THE UK

James Krabill and Stuart Murray, eds. *Forming Christian Habits in Post-Christendom: The Legacy of Alan and Eleanor Kreider*. Harrisonburg: Herald Press, 2011.

Alan Kreider and Stuart Murray, eds. *Coming Home: Stories of Anabaptists in Britian and Ireland*. Kitchener: Pandora Press, 2000.

Stuart Murray. *The Naked Anabaptist: Bare Essentials of a Radical Faith*. Scottdale: Herald Press, 2010. UK publication Paternoster Press, 2011; rev. ed. Herald Press, 2015.

ANABAPTIST HISTORY AND THEOLOGY

Brian C. Brewer, ed. *T&T Clark Handbook of Anabaptism*. London: T&T Clark, 2021.

William R. Estep. *The Anabaptist Story: An Introduction to Sixteenth-Century Anabaptism*. Grand Rapids: Eerdmans, 1996.

Thomas Finger. *A Contemporary Anabaptist Theology: Biblical, Historical, Constructive.* Downers Grove: IVP, 2004.

Walter Klaassen, ed. and trans. *Anabaptism in Outline: Selected Primary Sources.* Scottdale: Herald Press, 1981.

C. Arnold Snyder. *Anabaptist History and Theology: An Introduction.* Kitchener: Pandora Press, 1995.

MENNONITE BOOKS ON ANABAPTIST PRACTICES

David Augsburger. *Dissident Discipleship: A Spirituality of Self-Surrender, Love of God, and Love of Neighbor.* Grand Rapids: Brazos, 2006.

Palmer Becker. *Anabaptist Essentials: Ten Signs of a Unique Christian Faith.* Harrisonburg: Herald Press, 2017.

John D. Roth. *Practices: Mennonite Worship and Witness.* Scottdale: Herald Press, 2009.

C. Arnold Snyder. *Following in the Footsteps of Christ: The Anabaptist Tradition.* London: Darton, Longman & Todd, 2004.

ANABAPTIST BOOKS ON PEACE

J. Nelson Kraybill. *Stuck Together: The Hope of Christian Witness in a Polarized World.* Harrisonburg: Herald Press, 2023.

Alan Kreider, Eleanor Kreider, and Paulus Widjaja. *A Culture of Peace.* Intercourse: Good Books, 2005.

Osheta Moore. *Dear White Peacemakers: Dismantling Racism with Grit and Grace.* Harrisonburg: Herald Press, 2021.

John D. Roth. *Choosing against War: A Christian View.* Intercourse: Good Books, 2002.

ANABAPTIST BOOKS ON MISSION AND CHURCH

Colin Godwin. *Baptizing, Gathering, and Sending: Anabaptist Mission in the Sixteenth-Century Context.* Kitchener: Pandora Press, 2012.

Stanley Green and James Krabill, eds. *Fully Engaged: Missional Church in an Anabaptist Voice.* Harrisonburg: Herald Press, 2015.

Stuart Murray. *Post-Christendom: Church and Mission in a Strange New World.* Carlisle: Paternoster, 2004. Rev. ed. Wipf & Stock, 2017; SCM Press, 2018.

Stuart Murray Williams and Sian Murray Williams. *Multi-Voiced Church.* Milton Keynes: Paternoster, 2012.

WEBSITES

Anabaptism Today: AnabaptismToday.co.uk

Anabaptist Mennonite Network: AMNetwork.uk

Anabaptist Theology Forum: AMNetwork.uk/ Theology-Forum

Incarnate Network: AMNetwork.uk/Incarnate

Peaceful Borders: AMNetwork.uk/Peaceful-Borders

SoulSpace, Belfast: AMNetwork.uk/SoulSpace

SoulSpace, Bristol: SpaceForSoul.org.uk

Urban Expression: UrbanExpression.org.uk

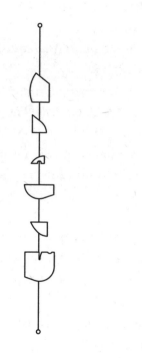

NOTES

INTRODUCTION

1. Named after the early Dutch Anabaptist leader Menno Simons, numerous Mennonite denominations in what is now a global movement relate together through the Mennonite World Conference.

2. The Anabaptist Network began in 1992. After a merger with the London Mennonite Trust, this is now the Anabaptist Mennonite Network. The network provides support and resources for the Anabaptist movement in the UK. To learn more, see AMNetwork.uk.

3. The term *post-Christendom* indicates that our society is emerging from the era of Christendom, when the church had political and social power, most people identified as Christian, and mission was understood as exporting Christianity to other parts of the world. In post-Christendom societies, many people know little or nothing of the Christian story, the churches are on the margins and much less influential, and mission includes creative engagement with our own plural culture.

4. Some American Mennonite friends suggested that the title may have been sufficiently titillating to increase sales in their communities, and I was amused to learn that at least one conservative book shop was unwilling to display a book with this title but kept copies under the counter for customers who requested it!

5. Stuart Murray, *The Naked Anabaptist: Bare Essentials of a Radical Faith* (Scottdale: Herald Press, 2010), 172. UK publication Paternoster Press, 2011; rev. ed. Herald Press, 2015.

6. Seventeen books have been published since 2004 and four more are under contract. These have been published by Paternoster Press, Herald Press, SCM Press, and Wipf & Stock.

7. For *Anabaptism Today*, see AnabaptismToday.co.uk. For the theology forum, see AnabaptistTheology.uk. For the Centre for Anabaptist Studies, go to https://www.bristol-baptist.ac.uk/study-centres/anabaptist-study-centre/.

8. The one exception was the Wood Green Mennonite Church, which emerged from the London Mennonite Centre and was integrally linked with the center. The closure of the center in 2010 soon resulted in the closure of the church.

9. For more information about Incarnate, see AMNetwork.uk/Planting and chapter 7 of this book.

10. Peaceful Borders, *Annual Report 2019*, last modified March 18, 2022, https://amnetwork.uk/wp-content/uploads/2020/04/2019-Annual-Report.pdf. For more information, see PeacefulBorders.org.

11. For more on Urban Expression, see UrbanExpression.org.uk.

12. See C. Arnold Snyder, *Following in the Footsteps of Christ: The Anabaptist Tradition* (London: Darton, Longman & Todd, 2004). A similar omission is apparent in Snyder's magisterial *Anabaptist History and Theology* (Kitchener: Pandora Press, 1995). See instead Colin Godwin, *Baptizing, Gathering, and Sending: Anabaptist Mission in the Sixteenth-Century Context* (Kitchener: Pandora Press, 2012).

13. See David Augsburger, *Dissident Discipleship: A Spirituality of Self-Surrender, Love of God, and Love of Neighbor* (Grand Rapids: Brazos, 2006).

14. John D. Roth, *Practices: Mennonite Worship and Witness* (Scottdale: Herald Press, 2009), 22.

15. See Palmer Becker, *Anabaptist Essentials: Ten Signs of a Unique Christian Faith* (Harrisonburg: Herald Press, 2017).

16. Roth, *Practices*, 220.

17. I am aware that this book will be marketed under my (male) name as a more established author known to the publisher, but these chapters enable three significant female voices to be heard. I have intentionally coauthored three previous books with women on ecclesial and missional subjects.

18. Examples are Harvey Kwiyani, *Sent Forth: African Missionary Work in the West* (Maryknoll: Orbis, 2014); and Israel Olofinjana, *World Christianity in Western Europe: Diasporic Identity, Narratives, and Missiology* (Minneapolis: Fortress Press, 2020).

19. See Drew G. I. Hart, *Trouble I've Seen: Changing the Way the Church Views Racism* (Harrisonburg: Herald Press, 2016), and *Who Will Be a Witness? Igniting Activism for God's Justice, Love, and Deliverance* (Harrisonburg: Herald Press, 2020); and Osheta Moore, *Dear White Peacemakers: Dismantling Racism with Grit and Grace* (Harrisonburg: Herald Press, 2021).

20. One of these, Gideon Diego, has reflected helpfully on Africa and the Anabaptist identity. See "As the Story Unfolds," *Anabaptism Today*, 21 September 2022, https://anabaptismtoday.co.uk/index.php/home/article/view/202.

21. See BlackLightCourse.uk.

22. See James Perkinson, *White Theology: Outing Supremacy in Modernity* (New York: Palgrave Macmillan, 2004).

23. The term *we* is used frequently throughout this book, usually referring to the Anabaptist Mennonite Network and indicating that I write from within a community.

CHAPTER 1

1. See Alan Kreider and Stuart Murray, eds., *Coming Home: Stories of Anabaptists in Britain and Ireland* (Kitchener: Pandora Press, 2000).

2. See further Palmer Becker, *Anabaptist Essentials: Ten Signs of a Unique Christian Faith* (Harrisonburg: Herald Press, 2017), 41–51. Becker also critiques dispensational and spiritualizing approaches.

3. See, for example, Helen Bond, *The Historical Jesus: A Guide for the Perplexed* (London: T&T Clark, 2012).

4. H. Wayne Pipkin and John Howard Yoder, trans. and ed., *Balthasar Hubmaier* (Scottdale: Herald Press, 1989), 180, 182. No reference to Yoder's work should now proceed without addressing his sexual abuse. A comprehensive account of his abuse and responses to it appears in Rachel Waltner Goossen, "'Defanging the Beast': Mennonite Responses to John Howard Yoder's Sexual Abuse," *Mennonite Quarterly Review* 89 (2015): 7–60.

5. See also Mark Bredin, *Jesus, Revolutionary of Peace: A Nonviolent Christology in the Book of Revelation* (Carlisle: Authentic Media, 2003).

6. See further James Stayer, *The German Peasants' War and Anabaptist Community of Good* (Montreal: McGill-Queen's University Press, 1991).

7. For a book-length treatment of this issue, see Stuart Murray, *Beyond Tithing* (Carlisle: Paternoster, 2000; Eugene: Wipf & Stock, 2012).

8. See also C. Arnold Snyder and Linda Huebert Hecht, *Profiles of Anabaptist Women* (Waterloo: Wilfrid Laurier University Press, 1996).

9. Quoted in Walter Klaassen, trans. and ed., *Anabaptism in Outline: Selected Primary Sources* (Scottdale: Herald Press, 1981), 87.

CHAPTER 2

1. Stuart Murray, *The Naked Anabaptist: Bare Essentials of a Radical Faith* (Scottdale: Herald Press, 2010), 112.

2. Quoted in Walter Klaassen, trans. and ed., *Anabaptism in Outline: Selected Primary Sources* (Scottdale: Herald Press, 1981), 167.

3. Palmer Becker, *Anabaptist Essentials: Ten Signs of a Unique Christian Faith* (Harrisonburg: Herald Press, 2017), 82. Becker gives examples of small groups in one Mennonite church asking each other searching questions about their use of time, talents, and money.

4. See Stuart Murray Williams and Sian Murray Williams, *Multi-Voiced Church* (Milton Keynes: Paternoster, 2012), 87–8. This book was also published as *The Power of All: Building a Multivoiced Church* (Scottdale: Herald Press, 2012).

5. See Shem Peachey, trans., and Paul Peachey, trans. and ed., "Answer of Some Who Are Called (Ana)baptists Why They Do Not Attend the Churches: A Swiss Brethren Tract," *Mennonite Quarterly Review* 45, no. 1 (1971): 10–11.

6. See Peacemeal.co, where it is clear that this term also applies more widely to other meals.

7. In C. S. Lewis, *The Lion, the Witch, and the Wardrobe* (London: Geoffrey Bles, 1950).

8. See C. Arnold Snyder, *Following in the Footsteps of Christ: The Anabaptist Tradition* (London: Darton, Longman & Todd, 2004), 104–8.

9. See Andrew Francis, *Hospitality and Community after Christendom* (Milton Keynes: Paternoster, 2012), 10. See also his *Eat, Pray, Tell: A Relational Approach to 21st-Century Mission* (Abingdon: Bible Reading Fellowship, 2018).

10. This understanding of communion nurtures the tripolar spirituality that David Augsburger commends. See Augsburger, *Dissident Discipleship: A Spirituality of Self-Surrender, Love of God, and Love of Neighbor* (Grand Rapids: Brazos, 2006).

11. Stuart Murray, *Naked Anabaptist*, 158. In *Practices: Mennonite Worship and Witness* (Scottdale: Herald Press, 2009), John D. Roth also reflects on the significance of shared meals in American Mennonite churches (115–17).

12. In an email forwarded to me by Mark Hurst on 29 January 2023.

13. Douglas Hynd, *Community Engagement after Christendom* (Eugene: Wipf & Stock, 2022), 154–201. See also Love Makes a Way Australia at https://actionnetwork.org/groups/love-makes-a-way-australia.

14. Letty Russell, *Just Hospitality: God's Welcome in a World of Difference* (Louisville: Westminster John Knox Press, 2009), 20.

15. Wesley used this phrase in a sermon preached on 27 June 1740, and on three other occasions. See further Dawn Chesser, "World Communion Sunday and Communion as Converting Ordinance," UMC Discipleship, 10 September 2013, https://www.umcdiscipleship.org/blog/world-communion-sunday-2013-and-communion-as-converting-ordinance.

CHAPTER 3

1. Stuart Murray Williams and Sian Murray Williams, *Multi-Voiced Church* (Milton Keynes: Paternoster, 2012), 46.

2. Steve Heinrichs, ed., *Unsettling the Word: Biblical Experiments in Decolonization* (Maryknoll: Orbis, 2019).

3. See Murray Williams and Murray Williams, *Multi-Voiced Church*.

4. Robert Greenleaf's seminal essay was "The Servant as Leader," but he wrote several books on the subject and founded the Greenleaf Center for Servant Leadership, which published his essay in 2012. Others developed James Downton's concept, and there is now a huge literature on both topics.

5. See, for example, Jimmy Long, *The Leadership Jump: Building Partnerships Between Existing and Emerging Christian Leaders* (Downers Grove: IVP, 2010).

6. *Anabaptism Today* featured articles on this subject with different perspectives by Lloyd Pietersen and Fran Porter. See Lloyd Pietersen, "Footwashing," *Anabaptism Today*, 2 November 2019, https://anabaptismtoday.co.uk/index.php/home/article/view/6; Fran Porter, "From Washing Feet to Shaking Hands," *Anabaptism Today*, 10 July 2020, https://anabaptismtoday.co.uk/index.php/home/article/view/60.

7. An extensive literature applies this concept to Christian leaders. A recent example is Hwa Yung, *Leadership or Servanthood? Walking in the Steps of Jesus* (Carlisle: Langham Global Library, 2021).

8. One of the earliest examples is Phillip Lewis, *Transformational Leadership: A New Model for Total Church Involvement* (Nashville: Broadman & Holman, 1996). The two terms may also be combined, as in Jeanine Parolini, *Transformational Servant Leadership* (Maitland: Xulon Press, 2012).

9. See Alan Kreider, "Abolishing the Laity," in *Anyone for Ordination?*, ed. Paul Beasley-Murray (Tunbridge Wells: MARC, 1993).

10. For some years, Urban Expression designated some of those working in local neighborhoods as "team leaders" and others as "team members," but this differentiation has been abolished. One of the coordinators is also recognized as the team leader, but she has no separate designation.

11. Observant readers might have noticed that this section is headed "shared leadership" rather than "nonhierarchical leadership." This change of terminology is partly in response to feedback from some who have argued that hierarchy is not inevitably harmful, illegitimate, or disempowering, and partly in order to emphasize a positive vision of shared leadership, rather than a critique of hierarchy.

12. Alexia Salvatierra and Brandon Wrencher, *Buried Seeds: Learning from the Vibrant Resilience of Marginalized Christian Communities* (Grand Rapids: Baker, 2022), 106.

13. See further Murray Williams and Murray Williams, *Multi-Voiced Church*, 105–23.

14. For the evidence, see Stuart Murray, *Biblical Interpretation in the Anabaptist Tradition* (Kitchener: Pandora Press, 2000), 157–85.

15. For an accessible account of this, see Anthony Arthur, *The Tailor-King: The Rise and Fall of the Anabaptist Kingdom of Münster* (New York: St. Martin's Press, 1999).

16. The full text can be found in *Mennonite Quarterly Review* 19 (October 1945), 247–53.

17. Christopher Landau, *A Theology of Disagreement: New Testament Ethics for Ecclesial Conflicts* (London: SCM Press, 2021).

18. Landau, 197.

19. Internal document endorsed by all who join Urban Expression.

20. J. Nelson Kraybill, *Stuck Together: The Hope of Christian Witness in a Polarized World* (Harrisonburg: Herald Press, 2023).

21. J. Richard Jackson, "The Church of the Bigger Table," *Post-Christendom Studies* 6 (2021–22), 87–105.

CHAPTER 4

1. Other examples include Isaiah 59:14–15; Jeremiah 5:1; 7:28; 9:5; Daniel 8:12; Amos 5:10.

2. "I swear that I will pay true allegiance to your majesty, and to your heirs and successors, according to law. So help me God."

3. Cited in Edmund Pries, "Anabaptist Oath Refusal: Basel, Bern and Strasbourg, 1525–1538" (PhD diss., University of Waterloo, 1995), 14–15. Recently published as Edmund Pries, *Anabaptist Oath Refusal: Basel, Bern, and Strasbourg, 1525–1538* (Kitchener: Pandora Press, 2023).

4. John D. Roth, *Practices: Mennonite Worship and Witness* (Scottdale: Herald Press, 2009), 71–73.

5. See, for example, Thomas Guthiel et al., "'The Whole Truth' versus 'The Admissible Truth': An Ethics Dilemma for Expert Witnesses," *Journal of the American Academy of Psychiatry and the Law* 31 (2003): 422–27.

6. See Alan Kreider and Eleanor Kreider, "Economical with the Truth: Swearing and Lying—An Anabaptist Perspective," *Brethren in Christ History and Life* 24 (2001):

152–77. This article charts the history of swearing oaths and resistance to the practice, and explores many aspects of truth-telling.

7. See Speak.org.uk.

8. In many of his writings, but see especially Walter Brueggemann, *The Prophetic Imagination* (Minneapolis: Fortress Press, 2018).

9. See PovertyTruthNetwork.org.

10. See, for example, Marlin Jeschke, *Discipling the Church: Recovering a Ministry of the Gospel* (Scottdale: Herald Press, 1989); C. Arnold Snyder, *Following in the Footsteps of Christ: The Anabaptist Tradition* (London: Darton, Longman & Todd, 2004), 86–90; Palmer Becker, *Anabaptist Essentials: Ten Signs of a Unique Christian Faith* (Harrisonburg: Herald Press, 2017), 125–35.

11. The practice of restorative justice will be explored in chapter 6.

CHAPTER 5

1. See further Lloyd Pietersen, *Reading the Bible after Christendom* (Milton Keynes: Paternoster, 2011).

2. See Bethany Dawson, "Many in the UK Face a Grim Choice This Winter," *Business Insider*, 9 October, 2022, https://www.businessinsider.com/cost-of-living-there-are-more-food-banks-mcdonalds-uk-2022-9.

3. While this chapter was being drafted, delegates at the COP27 climate conference finally agreed after decades of resistance to create a pooled fund for countries most affected by climate change in recognition of the responsibility of Western nations for the loss and damage caused over the past two centuries. Calls for reparations for the effects of the transatlantic slave trade continue.

4. Ronald Sider, *Living More Simply: Biblical Principles and Practices* (London: Hodder & Stoughton, 1980).

5. Ronald Sider, *Rich Christians in an Age of Hunger: Moving from Affluence to Generosity* (Downers Grove: IVP, 1977).

6. Evert van de Poll, "Making Virtue Out of Necessity: Energy, Inflation, Environmental Degradation, and the Call for Simpler Living," *Vista* 43 (March 2023): 3–4.

7. See Hutterites.org and Bruderhof.com.

8. See further, Stuart Murray, *Beyond Tithing* (Carlisle: Paternoster, 2000; Eugene: Wipf & Stock, 2012), 205–14.

9. See "Asset Based Community Development," Nurtured Development, 30 November 2011, https://www.nurturedevelopment.org/asset-based-community-development/.

CHAPTER 6

1. "Practicing peacemaking" was the original wording of this common practice, but I have added *nonviolent* in recognition that some other approaches to peacemaking involve violence.

2. In Mennonite Brethren circles, there is much less suspicion of the term *evangelism*.

3. See Alan Kreider, "Tongue Screws and Testimony," *Missio Dei* 16 (Elkhart: Mennonite Mission Network, 2008).

4. Her story is told in C. Arnold Snyder and Linda Huebert Hecht, eds., *Profiles of Anabaptist Women: Sixteenth-Century Reforming Pioneers* (Waterloo: Wilfrid Laurier University Press, 1996), 64–67.

5. Stanley Green and James Krabill, eds., *Fully Engaged: Missional Church in an Anabaptist Voice* (Harrisonburg: Herald Press, 2015).

6. Rick Richardson, "From the Will to Power to the Power of Weakness: Toward a Post-Christendom Evangelism," *Post-Christendom Studies* 5 (2020–21): 76, 100.

7. Alpha is a popular evangelistic course designed to introduce people to Christianity, combining shared food, presentations, and discussion. See Alpha.org.

8. Arthur McPhee, "Authentic Witness, Authentic Evangelism, Authentic Church," in *Evangelical, Ecumenical. and Anabaptist Missiologies in Conversation: Essays in Honor of Wilbert R. Shenk*, ed. James Krabill, Walter Sawatsky, and Charles van Engen (Maryknoll: Orbis, 2006), 133.

9. See Office for National Statistics, "Religion," Census 2021, accessed 28 August 2023, https://www.ons.gov.uk/peoplepopulationandcommunity/culturalidentity/religion.

10. See Paul Keeble, *Mission With: Something Out of the Ordinary* (Rickmansworth: Instant Apostle, 2017).

11. Stuart Murray, *The Naked Anabaptist: Bare Essentials of a Radical Faith* (Scottdale: Herald Press, 2010), 130.

12. Stuart Murray, *Naked Anabaptist*, 130–31.

13. See further RestorativeJustice.org.uk.

14. Christopher Marshall, *All Things Reconciled: Essays on Restorative Justice, Religious Violence, and the Interpretation of Scripture* (Eugene: Wipf & Stock, 2018).

15. Christopher Marshall, *Compassionate Justice: An Interdisciplinary Dialogue with Two Gospel Parables on Law, Crime, and Restorative Justice* (Eugene: Cascade, 2012).

16. Howard Zehr, *Changing Lenses: Restorative Justice for Our Times*, rev. ed. (Harrisonburg: Herald Press, 2015). Zehr is the author of several other books and guides on restorative justice, including *The Little Book of Restorative Justice* (Intercourse: Good Books, 2002).

17. See CommunityJusticeCenter.com.

18. See Office for National Statistics, "Religion."

19. Badru Kateregga and David W. Shenk, *A Muslim and a Christian in Dialogue* (Scottdale: Herald Press, 2011).

20. Gordon Nickel, *Peaceable Witness among Muslims* (Scottdale: Herald Press, 1999).

21. See Paulus Widjaja, "We Cannot Exist without the Other," Faith and Leadership, 15 August 2011, https://faithandleadership.com/paulus-widjaja-we-cannot-exist-without-the-other.

22. Jonathan Sacks, *Not in God's Name: Confronting Religious Violence* (London: Hodder and Stoughton, 2015). See further Susan Thistlethwaite, ed., *Interfaith Just Peacemaking* (New York: Palgrave Macmillan, 2011).

23. See further Israel Olofinjana, *World Christianity in Western Europe: Diasporic Identity, Narratives, and Missiology* (Minneapolis: Fortress Press, 2020); and Harvey Kwiyani, *Sent Forth: African Missionary Work in the West* (Maryknoll: Orbis, 2014).

24. See CrucibleCourse.org.uk.

25. See BBMinistries.org.uk and a book by the former director, Alastair McKay, *Bridgebuilding: Making Peace with Conflict in the Church* (London: Canterbury Press, 2019).

26. The booklet by Alan Kreider and Eleanor Kreider, *Becoming a Peace Church* (London: Anabaptist Network, 2000), and course can be accessed at https://amnetwork.uk/resource/becoming-a-peace-church-study-guide/.

27. Alan Kreider, Eleanor Kreider, and Paulus Widjaja, *A Culture of Peace: God's Vision for the Church* (Intercourse: Good Books, 2005).

28. Osheta Moore, *Dear White Peacemakers: Dismantling Racism with Grit and Grace* (Harrisonburg: Herald Press, 2021).

CHAPTER 7

1. See, for example, Stefan Paas, *Church Planting in the Secular West: Learning from the European Experience* (Grand Rapids: Eerdmans, 2016).

2. On the history of the early years of the Bruderhof community in the UK, see Ian Randall, *A Christian Peace Experiment: The Bruderhof Community in Britain, 1933–1942* (Eugene: Cascade Books, 2018).

3. Based in the United States, the Brethren in Christ Church denomination emerged from Mennonite roots and has also been shaped by radical pietism and the holiness tradition.

4. The three core values of Urban Expression are relationship, creativity, and humility. The seven commitments are being on the margins, being Jesus-centered, committing to the shalom vision of peace, seeking the kingdom of God, nurturing uncluttered church, serving unconditionally, and building respectful relationships with all people.

5. The preexisting Incarnate Network was a primarily Baptist initiative. But it shared an ethos and a number of values with the Anabaptist Mennonite Network's church planting initiative, so when the Incarnate Network was looking for a more sustainable organizational basis for the future, it was decided to amalgamate with the AMN. Incarnate was adopted as the name for this new Anabaptist church planting initiative.

6. "Incarnate," Anabaptist Mennonite Network, accessed 10 May 2023, https://amnetwork.uk/incarnate/.

7. Godly Play uses wondering questions, storytelling, and creativity to help children to explore Christian themes through their own experiences. "Godly Play begins with children's innate sense of the presence of God. It offers Christian language as a support for their ongoing spiritual formation." "Godly Play UK," accessed 28 August 2023, https://www.godlyplay.uk/

8. Rachel Haig, "SoulSpace Bristol: An Attempt at Incarnation," *Anabaptism Today*, 24 April 2023, https://anabaptismtoday.co.uk/index.php/home/article/view/227/.

9. "Everyone Belongs: Weekly Summary," Center for Action and Contemplation, 29 January 2022, https://cac.org/daily-meditations/everyone-belongs-weekly-summary-2022-01-29/, based on "Diversity Welcome," Training for Change, last modified 3 July 2023, https://www.trainingforchange.org/training_tools/diversity-welcome/.

10. This terminology was introduced by Anabaptist missiologist Paul Hiebert in his *Anthropological Reflections on Missiological Issues* (Grand Rapids: Baker Academic, 1994). See further Mark Baker, *Centered-Set Church: Discipleship and Community without Judgmentalism* (Downers Grove: IVP Academic, 2022).

CHAPTER 8

1. Crawford Gribben, *The Rise and Fall of Christian Ireland* (Oxford: Oxford University Press, 2021), 2.

2. Gribben, 3.

3. The Irish Inter-Church Meeting, *The Dearest Freshness Deep Down Things* (Belfast: Irish Inter-Church Meeting, 2005), 29, http://www.irishchurches.org/cmsfiles/resources/Reports/DFDDT.pdf.

4. C. Arnold Snyder, *Anabaptist History and Theology* (Kitchener: Pandora Press, 1995), 2.

5. Snyder, 1.

6. Snyder, 116.

7. Karen Sethuraman, "There's Always a Place for Those Who Don't Belong," 17 September 2022, https://belfastmedia.com/rev-karen-there-s-always-a-place-for-those-who-don-t-belong.

8. The slogan "For God and Ulster" speaks to Protestant and unionist opposition to the demands of Irish nationalists and republicans.

9. See further Rachel Haig, "SoulSpace Bristol: An Attempt at Incarnation," *Anabaptism Today*, 24 April 2023, https://anabaptismtoday.co.uk/index.php/home/article/view/227/.

10. Andrew Davison and Alison Milbank, *For the Parish: A Critique of Fresh Expressions* (London: SCM Press, 2010).

11. Walter Klaassen, *Anabaptism: Neither Catholic nor Protestant* (Waterloo: Conrad Press, 1973), 9.

CHAPTER 9

1. Juliet Kilpin, *Urban to the Core: Motives for Urban Mission* (Eugene: Wipf & Stock, 2014). The values can also be explored further through the Urban Expression website and liturgy. See UrbanExpression.org.uk.

2. ITV News, "David Cameron: 'Swarm' of Migrants Crossing Mediterranean," BBC, 30 July 2015, 0:33, https://www.bbc.co.uk/news/av/uk-politics-33714282.

3. Compagnies Républicaines de Sécurité (a section of the police involved in security enforcement).

4. International Rescue Committee, "What Is the Dubs Amendment?," Rescue, 6 February 2000, www.rescue.org/uk/article/what-dubs-amendment.

CONCLUSION

1. Alan and Eleanor Kreider in the UK, Mark and Mary Hurst in Australia, Andrew and Karen Suderman in South Africa, and several others.

2. In an email dated 17 June 2015.

3. Quoted in Walter Klaassen, trans. and ed., *Anabaptism in Outline: Selected Primary Sources* (Scottdale: Herald Press, 1981), 75.

4. Arthur Paul Boers et al., comps., *Take Our Moments and Our Days: An Anabaptist Prayer Book*, vol. 1., *Ordinary Time* (Scottdale: Herald Press, 2007), vol. 2., *Advent through Pentecost* (Scottdale: Herald Press, 2010).

5. See Daniel Liechty, *Early Anabaptist Spirituality: Selected Writings* (New York: Paulist Press, 1994); Marlene Kropf and Eddy Hall, *Praying with the Anabaptists: The Secret of Bearing Fruit* (Newton: Faith & Life Press, 1994); Leonard Gross, trans. and ed., *Prayer Book for Earnest Christians: A Spiritually Rich Anabaptist Resource* (Scottdale: Herald Press, 1997); Colin Godwin, *Anabaptist Meditations: Thirty Days of Biblical Reflection from the Founders of the Tradition* (Kitchener: Pandora Press, 2022).

6. Other suggestions, most of them not serious, included "Clothing the Naked Anabaptist," "Anabaptist Foundation Garments," "The Semi-clothed Anabaptist," "The Not-so-Naked Anabaptist," "The Rather Chilly Anabaptist," and "Anabaptist Underwear"!

7. In Luther's preface to his commentary on the Sermon on the Mount.

8. Ulrich Zwingli, "Of Baptism," in *Zwingli and Bullinger*, ed. G. W. Bromiley (London: SCM Press, 1953), 148.

9. Michael Sattler, "The Capito Letters" (1527), in *The Legacy of Michael Sattler*, ed. John Howard Yoder (Scottdale: Herald Press, 1973), 87.

10. Dietrich Bonhoeffer, writing to his brother Karl Friedrich, 14 January 1935.

11. Andrew Walker, *Telling the Story: Gospel, Mission, and Culture* (London: SPCK, 1996), 190.

12. John D. Roth, *Practices: Mennonite Worship and Witness* (Scottdale: Herald Press, 2009), 85.

13. James Krabill and Stuart Murray, eds., *Forming Christian Habits in Post-Christendom* (Harrisonburg: Herald Press, 2011), 35.

14. Dorothy Bass and Craig Dykstra, *Practicing Our Faith: A Way of Life for a Searching People* (San Francisco: Jossey-Bass, 1997), 8. The twelve practices are honoring the body, hospitality, household economics, saying yes and saying no, keeping the Sabbath, testimony, discernment, shaping communities, forgiveness, healing, dying well, and singing our lives. Other writers explore the impact of focal practices, the cultivation of virtues, and the influence of core values.

15. See Stuart Murray, *The Naked Anabaptist: Bare Essentials of a Radical Faith* (Scottdale: Herald Press, 2010), 109–10.

APPENDIX 3

1. This stanza by an anonymous source is found in David Adam, *The Open Gate: Celtic Prayers for Growing Spirituality* (London: SPCK, 2006), 80. The origin of the second stanza is unknown.

CONTRIBUTORS

South African by birth, **Alexandra Ellish** spent her teenage years in England and then studied theology in Edinburgh and later Prague, where she was ordained as a Baptist minister. Alex has been engaged in urban mission and ministry since 2009 as a local church leader, Urban Expression mission partner, and coordinator. Alex chairs the Incarnate church planting steering group of the Anabaptist Mennonite Network. She has training in pastoral supervision and supports Baptist ministers in training. Alex lives with her husband Philip, their two children, and an affable Jack Russell in Peckham, South London, where she is also the minister of Amott Road Baptist Church. Alex has itchy feet and dreams about all the places she might one day live, but in the meantime, she enjoys the eclectic and delicious food of South London, meeting interesting people, and playing football with her local team.

Juliet Kilpin is a cofounder and coordinator of Peaceful Borders, a project of the Anabaptist Mennonite Network. Prior to this, she cofounded and coordinated Urban Expression, an urban mission initiative that began in 1997. Juliet studied and taught at Spurgeon's College and has been a Baptist minister since 1996. She is also a senior community organizer with Citizens UK, a people-powered alliance dedicated to challenging injustice and building stronger communities. She is currently chair of the European Baptist Federation's Commission on Migration.

Karen Sethuraman is the first female Baptist minister in Ireland. She is currently a pastor of SoulSpace, Peace and Reconciliation hub. Karen feels particularly called to minister outside the church walls, journeying with people who feel they don't fit in church. She has served as chaplain to two Belfast Lord Mayors and is currently on the executive committee of the Northern Ireland Interfaith Forum. She also writes a weekly column for *Belfast Media* and is part of the Ireland's Future team.

Stuart Murray, a freelance trainer and consultant, was one of the founders of the Anabaptist Mennonite Network. He is the director of the Centre for Anabaptist Studies at Bristol Baptist College and has a PhD in Anabaptist hermeneutics. He was also one of the founders of Urban Expression, an Anabaptist-oriented urban mission agency. He is the editor of the After Christendom series and has written books on urban mission, church planting, post-Christendom, hermeneutics, and Anabaptism, including *The Naked Anabaptist*.